LOCKE:
A GUIDE FOR THE PERPLEXED

Continuum Guides for the Perplexed

Continuum's Guides for the Perplexed are clear, concise, and accessible introductions to thinkers, writers, and subjects that students and readers can find especially challenging. Concentrating specifically on what it is that makes the subject difficult to grasp, these books explain and explore key themes and ideas, guiding the reader toward a thorough understanding of demanding material.

***Guides for the Perplexed* available from Continuum:**
Adorno: A Guide for the Perplexed, Alex Thomson
Arendt: A Guide for the Perplexed, Karin Fry
Aristotle: A Guide for the Perplexed, John Vella
Bentham: A Guide for the Perplexed, Philip Schofield
Berkley: A Guide for the Perplexed, Talia Bettcher
Deleuze: A Guide for the Perplexed, Claire Colebrook
Derrida: A Guide for the Perplexed, Julian Wolfreys
Descartes: A Guide for the Perplexed, Justin Skirry
The Empiricists: A Guide for the Perplexed, Laurence Carlin
Existentialism: A Guide for the Perplexed, Stephen Earnshaw
Freud: A Guide for the Perplexed, Celine Surprenant
Gadamer: A Guide for the Perplexed, Chris Lawn
Habermas: A Guide for the Perplexed, Lasse Thomassen
Hegel: A Guide for the Perplexed, David James
Heidegger: A Guide for the Perplexed, David Cerbone
Hobbes: A Guide for the Perplexed, Stephen J. Finn
Hume: A Guide for the Perplexed, Angela Coventry
Husserl: A Guide for the Perplexed, Matheson Russell
Kant: A Guide for the Perplexed, TK Seung
Kierkegaard: A Guide for the Perplexed, Clare Carlisle
Leibniz: A Guide for the Perplexed, Franklin Perkins
Levinas: A Guide for the Perplexed, B.C. Hutchens
Merleau-Ponty: A Guide for the Perplexed, Eric Matthews
Nietzsche: A Guide for the Perplexed, R. Kevin Hill
Plato: A Guide for the Perplexed, Gerald A. Press
Pragmatism: A Guide for the Perplexed, Robert B. Talisse and Scott F. Aikin
Quine: A Guide for the Perplexed, Gary Kemp
Relativism: A Guide for the Perplexed, Timothy Mosteller
Ricoeur: A Guide for the Perplexed, David Pellauer
Rousseau: A Guide for the Perplexed, Matthew Simpson
Sartre: A Guide for the Perplexed, Gary Cox
Socrates: A Guide for the Perplexed, Sara Ahbel-Rappe
Spinoza: A Guide for the Perplexed, Charles Jarrett
The Stoics: A Guide for the Perplexed, M. Andrew Holowchak
Utilitarianism: A Guide for the Perplexed, Krister Bykvist

LOCKE:
A GUIDE FOR THE PERPLEXED

PATRICIA SHERIDAN

continuum

Continuum International Publishing Group
The Tower Building   80 Maiden Lane
11 York Road   Suite 704
London SE1 7NX   New York NY 10038

www.continuumbooks.com

© Patricia Sheridan 2010

All rights reserved. No part of this publication may be reproduced or
transmitted in any form or by any means, electronic or mechanical,
including photocopying, recording, or any information storage or retrieval
system, without prior permission in writing from the publishers.

British Library Cataloguing-in-Publication Data
A catalogue record for this book is available from the British Library.

ISBN: HB: 978-0-8264-8983-8
PB: 978-0-8264-8984-5

Library of Congress Cataloguing-in-Publication Data
Sheridan, Patricia.
Locke—a guide for the perplexed / Patricia Sheridan.
p. cm.
Includes bibliographical references and index.
ISBN-13: 978-0-8264-8983-8 (HB)
ISBN-10: 0-8264-8983-4 (HB)
ISBN-13: 978-0-8264-8984-5 (pbk.)
ISBN-10: 0-8264-8984-2 (pbk.)
1. Locke, John, 1632–1704. I. Title.
B1297.S47 2010
192—dc22

2009022135

Typeset by Newgen Imaging Systems Pvt Ltd, Chennai, India
Printed and bound in Great Britain by CPI Antony Rowe,
Chippenham, Wiltshire

CONTENTS

INTRODUCTION

Locke's *Essay Concerning Human Understanding*, published in 1690, is a *tour de force*—it is an ambitious work, devoted to constructing a foundational theory of knowledge, of language, and of the nature and origin of ideas. But the expansiveness of its subject matter, combined with the sometimes painstaking detail of its discussions, can make it a challenging work to read. The diverse and sometimes sprawling discussions of the *Essay* can tend to obscure the thematic coherence of the project as a whole. It is therefore useful, at the outset, to try to identify the general theme of the work, and Locke gave us some clues to that effect in his introductory *Epistle to the Reader*. Unfortunately, Locke does not straightforwardly state what his primary concern is, and he manages to offer us two somewhat different versions of his motivation for writing the *Essay*. Despite this, there is a general point of view regarding knowledge that is prominent in both accounts, and which brings all the pieces of Locke's work into focus.

In an oft-quoted section of the *Epistle*, Locke describes the ambition of his work as the modest one of serving natural science. He describes himself as privileged to be *"employed as an Under-Labourer in clearing the Ground a little, and removing some of the Rubbish, that lies in the way to Knowledge"* (*Epistle*, 10). The frequent appeal to various principles of natural science throughout the text, combined with Locke's self-characterization as "under-labourer" to the sciences, has led some readers to presume that the primary goal of the *Essay* is to construct a theory of ideas that supports and defends modern scientific methods. There is no doubt that much of the *Essay* is intended as a means of accomplishing this end; however, we risk misunderstanding the intent of the *Essay* if we read Locke's work solely in this light. Though Locke's work is clearly motivated by his interests in modern science, the *Essay* also devotes significant space to questions of moral and religious knowledge. Unless we wish to dismiss these topics as being only tangential to Locke's natural scientific commitments—and there is little reason to do so—we need to understand the scope of the *Essay* in somewhat broader terms.

In the course of the *Epistle*, Locke famously recounts another source of inspiration for writing the *Essay*. He explains that his interest in writing the *Essay* was stirred by a discussion one evening with several of his friends, on subjects that Locke identifies only as being *"very remote"* from the topic of the *Essay* (though James Tyrell, one of the friends in attendance that evening, later identified their topics of discussion as morality and religion). After a lengthy debate, Locke recounts, their discourse came to a standstill when they realized they were dealing with issues so dense and complicated that no resolution was forthcoming. As Locke recalls,

> it came into my Thoughts, that we took a wrong course; and that, before we set our selves upon Enquiries of that Nature, it was necessary to examine our own Abilities, and see, what Objects our Understandings were, or were not fitted to deal with. (*Epistle*, 7)

Morality and religion also have a place beside natural science as subjects explored at significant length in the *Essay*, yet the inspiration for the *Essay* should not be sought in one specific subject. Locke's motivating concern can be discerned by paying close attention to the more general question Locke raises in the quote above. Locke's overriding interest in the *Essay* is not to lay foundations for any specific discipline; Locke aims to examine the nature of inquiry, its foundations, its standards for truth, and the means we have for improving systematic investigations of all kinds. For Locke, success in any intellectual undertaking, be it natural science, morality, or religion, depends upon having a fundamental grasp of the origin and nature of knowledge itself. Locke thus calls for a proper accounting of our ideas and the relations that can reasonably be drawn between them. In this way, we may avoid the pitfalls of aiming at certainty where there is only probability, or claiming knowledge where there is none to be had. As Locke puts this in Book I of the *Essay*, "It is therefore worth while, to search out the *Bounds* between Opinion and Knowledge; and examine by what Measures, in things, whereof we have no certain Knowledge, we ought to regulate our Assent, and moderate our Perswasions"

(1.1.3). The enterprise of examining the origin and content of our ideas is ultimately aimed at establishing what our minds are capable of knowing and setting appropriate standards for truth. As Locke sees it, the problems that inhibit real learning arise from a failure to appreciate this; assertions that exceed the boundaries of human ideas and reason lead us into irresolvable debate as well as pernicious overconfidence.

Locke frequently refers to the fittedness or suitableness of our minds to certain kinds of inquiry; he thinks our minds are fashioned such that we may gain knowledge in degrees appropriate to our human needs. He does not, therefore, think we ought to hold all of our inquiries to the same standard of knowledge; for Locke, the relative potential for knowledge in our scientific, moral, and religious pursuits depends on the ideas we have and what these ideas are taken to represent. For Locke, the contents of thought, our ideas, originate in experience. As a result, whatever we can conclude about the world is limited to our experiences; for Locke, most of these ideas are necessarily incomplete—we can have no ideas of the world as it exists beyond our perceptual experience. Locke offers us a humbled conception of scientific knowledge. This might seem to be an odd conclusion for a thinker who seeks to provide an epistemological foundation for science. However, Locke's task is not to undermine science, but to instill an appropriate modesty in our approach to scientific theory, consistent with the Baconian program. Modern science, as Bacon conceived it, is predicated on limits—hypotheses need constant testing, and hopefully, perfecting, with the goal not of absolute truths, but of useful and practical outcomes for human life. In this same spirit, Locke explores the limits of scientific understanding, and sets out to establish appropriate standards for the justification of our scientific beliefs. As we will see, Locke also seeks to mark out relatively appropriate standards for moral and religious knowledge.

Locke spends a great deal of time pointing out the gaps in, and inadequacies of, experiential ideas. However, Locke's view is not a call for skepticism. In defining the limits of knowledge, Locke emphasizes the proper appreciation of what we *need* to know to live well. Locke's epistemology is pragmatic; though many things cannot be known with certainty, we do, he thinks, have the tools necessary for achieving a level of assurance, with regard to the truth or falsity of our beliefs, that is adequate to living well and happily. As

Locke sees it, then, inquiry does not have to aim at absolute truths and certainties, but at providing the greatest possible knowledge that will serve the requirements of life, whether in natural science, religion, or morality. In the *Epistle*, Locke states that despite the critical response his work will generate, he will *"always have the satisfaction to have aimed at Truth and Usefulness"* (*Epistle*, 9). To this end, Locke sets out to examine knowledge itself—not only its limits and extent, but also its origin in experience. With its emphasis on the perils of dogmatism and superstition, the *Essay* sought to lay the groundwork for a kind of intellectual accountability that would not only free rational individuals from religious, political, and intellectual oppression, but also encourage them to embrace their responsibilities as rational agents to use reason in guiding them to the best possible life. As Locke explains, humans have been given "Whatsoever is necessary for the Conveniences of Life, and Information of Virtue; and [God] has put within the reach of their Discovery the comfortable provision for this Life and the Way that leads to a better" (1.1.5). Certainty with regard to many things will elude us. But to disdain our limits and cast doubt on whatever cannot be known with certainty is to misunderstand the practical function of knowledge and to extol only that kind of knowledge that reaches to the lofty heights of abstraction and absolute truth.

Locke's early experiences at Oxford and the acquaintances he made there had a formative influence on his work. It is, therefore, useful, by way of introduction, to understand something of Locke's life and career.

BIOGRAPHY

Locke was born in Somerset, England, on August 28, 1632. His father, John Locke senior, was a landowner, attorney, and minor Government administrator. During the English Civil War, Locke's father fought on the side of Parliament under Alexander Popham, a member of the Somerset gentry who became a member of parliament after the war. Locke senior maintained his connection with Popham, whose influence allowed him to recommend young John Locke to Westminster School, one of the leading schools in England at that time. Here Locke gained a first-class education and was eventually elected to Christ Church, Oxford in 1652.

Oxford at this time was dominated by the Aristotelianism of the Middle Ages, and students followed a standard curriculum of logic, metaphysics, and classical languages leading to a Bachelor of Arts degree. Like his predecessor the famed philosopher Thomas Hobbes, Locke found the curriculum of Oxford tremendously outdated, and, in the words of Hobbes years earlier, the philosophy taught was "Aristotelity," with no emphasis on original thought but "rigide truth."[1] Though Oxford may not have been quite so dogmatically devoted to Aristotelianism as Hobbes suggests, there seems to have been some intellectual divide in this period between the Aristotelians and those embracing the new wave of ideas emerging at this time. Locke himself was no doubt recalling his days at Oxford in his numerous characterizations of "the Schools" as institutions of pointless disputation over befuddling terminology. As he charges in Book III, the Schoolmen dispute obscure terminology rather than aiming at discovering new or useful knowledge for humankind. Locke describes them in the following glowing terms:

> aiming at Glory and Esteem, for their great and universal Knowledge, easier a great deal to be pretended to, than really acquired, found this a good Expedient to cover their Ignorance, with a curious and inexplicable Web of perplexed Words, and procure to themselves the admiration of others, by unintelligible Terms, the apter to produce wonder, because they could not be understood, whilst it appears in all History that these profound Doctors were no wiser, nor more useful than their Neighbours; and brought but small advantage to humane Life, or the Societies wherein they lived. (3.10.8)

This "learned ignorance" (3.10.10), as Locke calls it, was, if not the only intellectual activity at Oxford, at least predominant enough to have concerned modern thinkers such as Locke and Hobbes.

The intellectual environment of Oxford was changing in the seventeenth century. The English Royal Society was founded at Oxford by John Wilkins. Wilkins gathered a group of intellectuals dedicated to the principles of a burgeoning new science devoted to the Baconian enterprise of founding science in the "historical" method of experimentation and hypothesis. Locke was introduced to the ideas of this society through his friend Richard Lower, and his interest in new approaches to medicine and natural science grew. Robert Boyle eventually took over as the leading voice of the society. Locke was closely association with Boyle, and was thereby exposed to Boyle's groundbreaking theoretical work on atomistic mechanism. Throughout his life, Locke was devoted to the work of the great names in modern science, working closely with Boyle and developing friendships with Sydenham, Huygens, and Newton.

During his earlier days at Oxford, Locke explored the possibility of pursuing the law, ordination into the ministry, and medicine. His detailed notes indicate he was reading a great number of medical works through the 1650s, most notably Harvey's groundbreaking work on the circulation of the blood. In the 1660s, Locke was appointed to several college offices, eventually becoming a college tutor. Throughout this period, Locke was engaging in informal studies in medicine, having decided to become a physician. Locke even set up a laboratory at Oxford to study medicine and anatomy. At this time Locke was also busy developing his political views, penning early tracts on the authority of the state vis-à-vis the individual and on religious toleration. In the early 1660s, Locke wrote what is now known as the *Two Tracts on Government*. His interest in moral philosophy was also developing at this time, and he penned a then-unpublished work which has come to be known as the *Essays on the Law of Nature*.

It was at this time that Locke established his friendship with Anthony Ashley Cooper, one of the wealthiest men in England, and an important politician, who would be enormously influential in Locke's life. Cooper was unwell and arrived at Oxford to take the medicinal waters there. In 1667, Cooper invited Locke to live with him as his personal physician, secretary, and researcher. Locke left Oxford and lived with Lord Ashley for the next eight years, firmly establishing himself as Lord Ashley's friend. In 1668, he diagnosed an abscess on Lord Ashley's liver and recommended life-saving surgery.

During his years in Lord Ashley's residence, Locke was not only devoted to the study of modern science, but also continued his work on political theory. In 1667, he wrote the *Essay Concerning Toleration*. At this time, Locke was chiefly involved in helping Lord Ashley in establishing trade with the colonies, particularly with regard to founding colonies in the Carolinas. Locke was deeply involved in drafting the constitution of the Carolinas, and writing documents regarding other public policy issues such as the monetary situation in England. Lord Ashley was eventually forced to flee England for the more politically tolerant Holland, after terms of imprisonment in the Tower of London. Ashley had been strongly opposed to the succession to the throne of the Catholic brother of Charles II. He had been active in supporting the exclusion bill that would have prevented this succession. The rising tensions between Protestant and Catholic parties made the situation in England sufficiently threatening that Locke followed Lord Ashley to Holland in 1683.

It was in Holland that Locke finished his work *An Essay on Toleration*, along with the *Essay Concerning Human Understanding*. By this time, Locke had also befriended a number of English revolutionaries in exile. The English Government attempted to extradite a number of them back to England, including Locke. Charles II was eventually succeeded by his Catholic brother, James II, who was forced to flee to France in the face of mounting opposition, culminating in the arrival, in 1688, of a revolutionary force led by the Protestant William of Orange. This was known as the Glorious Revolution. This event marked the change in power from king to Parliament, and had enormous implications for the political climate of England.

Locke returned to England in 1688, and soon after published the *Essay Concerning Human Understanding* and *The Two Treatises of Government*. For the remaining years of his life, Locke lived with his long-time friend, and one-time romantic interest, Damarais Masham and her husband Sir Francis Masham. Here Locke enjoyed a lively intellectual friendship with Lady Masham, as well as entertaining many of the luminaries of his day. Locke died on October 28, 1704.

CHAPTER ONE

LOCKE'S THEORY OF IDEAS

Locke's goal in Books I and II is to examine the content of human consciousness and the origin of ideas, but his project is not to produce a mere taxonomy. Locke's intent is to rethink traditional conceptions of knowledge and intellectual accountability. What we see Locke objecting to, time and again, in Book I is the all-too-common tendency people have to accept the truth of traditional principles regarding religion, morality, and the natural sciences without paying sufficient attention to the degree of their evidentiary support. Locke saw a great danger in accepting as true what one takes on authority alone, and sought to turn the attention of philosophy to knowledge itself and the proper methods for discovering truth.

BOOK I: LOCKE'S ARGUMENT AGAINST INNATE IDEAS

Book I can be read as a kind of ground-clearing for Locke's project in the subsequent three books of the *Essay*. Where Books II–IV deal with aspects of Locke's positive theory of ideas, Book I concentrates on the view of ideas which Locke presumably considered his main foil—the theory of innate ideas. To understand the view that Locke is attacking in Book I, it is useful to consider the innatist assertions found in the writing of leading theologians and philosophers of Locke's day.

Innatist thinkers generally believed that the knowledge of God and of our moral duties (among other things) resides in the mind from birth. There were stronger and weaker versions of this position in the air in the seventeenth century. The stronger position can be characterized as the naïve theory of innateness, according to which there are a number of principles stamped on the mind at birth, or, as it was commonly expressed, *written into the hearts of men*. These innate principles typically included the fundamentals of religious belief, mathematical axioms, and a host of commonly held moral propositions. The naïve position was rejected by a number of people at the time, who proposed a somewhat toned-down version of the innate ideas thesis. This more moderate view does not hold that propositions are actually resident in the mind, but rather that the mind seems predisposed to recognize the truth of certain propositions in the manner of a kind of recollection. Bishop Edward Stillingfleet, who was a famous interlocutor of Locke's, argued that the widespread belief in God's existence (and particularly the readiness of assent among people who had not formerly been exposed to the notion) suggests that *"God has stamped a universal character of himself upon the minds of Men."*[1] Stillingfleet identifies two specific conditions under which a proposition may be considered innate: "1. *If it be such as bears the same importance among all person. 2. If it be such as cannot be mistaken for the character of any thing else."*[2] For Stillingfleet, the universality and clarity of certain propositions was evidence that they were, at the very least, familiar to human reason. Henry More, who was one of the great intellectuals of his day, held that the mind is, as it were, pre-programmed to recognize true propositions when presented with them; much as one remembers a tune when one hears the first few notes, these ideas are, according to More, triggered or awakened by experience. Propositions he has in mind include geometrical truths, such as "the whole is bigger than the part" or "the three angles in a triangle are equal to two right ones." Ralph Cudworth, another important thinker of the seventeenth century, held that reason has an innate grasp of the principles of natural science. Cudworth argued that empirical observation cannot discover the essence of things in the world, which he took to be the great end of scientific inquiry. Rather, essences are discovered by looking inward, reflecting on what the intellect already, in some sense, knows; essences are characters written into the intellect. He explained as follows:

> As to the universal and abstract theorems of science, the terms whereof are those reasons of things, which exist no where but only in the mind itself (whose noemata and ideas they are) the measure and rule of truth concerning them can be no foreign or extraneous thing without the mind, but must be native and

domestic to it, or contained within the mind itself, and therefore can be nothing but its clear and distinct perception.[3]

He continues in this vein, explaining that while the senses can perceive individual objects in the world, "abstract universal rationes, reasons, are that higher station of the mind, from whence looking down upon individual things, it hath a commanding view of them, and as it were a priori comprehends or knows them."[4] Many thinkers in Locke's day held some brand of innate ideas theory. But it was commonly believed by naïve and moderate innatists alike that reason was like a light or candle in each and every one of us, containing, in some sense, all the most basic principles of natural and moral philosophy, which were just waiting to be teased out by experience. Reason was seen as a storehouse of knowledge, cognizant of true propositions prior to, and thus independently of, experiential data. Experience could act as a catalyst for bringing this knowledge to consciousness, but it was not seen as its origin. As John Smith, another Cambridge Platonist wrote,

> There are some radical principles of knowledge that are so deeply sunk into the souls of men, as that the impression cannot easily be obliterated, though it may be much darkened . . . [it] hath well observed, that the common notions of God and virtue impressed upon the souls of men, are more clear and perspicuous than any else.[5]

Typically, the proponents of innate ideas appealed to the divine origin of these ideas as a basis for their legitimacy. This succeeded in making such ideas beyond reproach and immune to critical scrutiny. It also had the effect of giving supposedly innate propositions the status of axiomatic principles on which to found metaphysical and moral doctrines.

Locke would have been very familiar with this kind of reasoning, and saw in it the seeds for error and dogmatism of the very worst kind. The doctrine of innate ideas signaled for him a defense of intellectual authoritarianism; as Locke warns, the teacher of absolute truths can "make a Man swallow that for innate Principles, which may serve to his purpose, who teacheth them" (1.4.24). Whereas, he continues, if the foundations of knowledge were properly examined by each person, the principles once taken to be authoritative by their innateness would be discovered as having sprung from "the minds of Men, from the being of things themselves" (1.4.24). True learning, for Locke, happens only once practical and speculative principles are properly understood as arising from the workings of human reason on the ideas of experience. Critical analysis and intellectual accountability would follow, he believed, once the veil of intellectual absolutism was drawn back. Locke sought to put forward a more rigorous foundation for the assertion and analysis of knowledge claims.

Locke's method is at turns destructive and reconstructive. Book I exposes the tenuous claims made in support of innate principles of knowledge; Book II seeks to establish the foundations for a new approach to questions of truth and knowledge. First and foremost, he aims to show that reason does not contain propositions innately, nor is the mind in any sense cognizant of them prior to the workings of reason upon our ideas.

In Book I, Locke takes aim at two kinds of propositions: speculative and practical. Speculative propositions are those dealing with abstract mathematical principles; practical propositions are general principles of theology and morality. Locke sets out to show that the alleged innateness of these propositions rests on two mistaken assumptions: that they are universally known, and that they are recognizable as self-evident to any rational person. It is, Locke explains, common for innatists to point to the universality of consent to certain propositions. Consider the following proposition, which would fall under Locke's heading of speculative principles: *The three angles of a triangle are equal to two right ones.* No one doubts the truth of this claim, so the innatist argument would go, and so we can say with a fair amount of confidence that this is universally agreed to be true. If every person can see the truth of this proposition, then we can fairly assume that the proposition represents innate knowledge. The conclusion the innatist draws, as we have seen, is that such propositions are so readily understood that they must be ideas the mind, in some sense, already knew or recognized to be true.

What does Locke say to this line of reasoning? He argues that it does not follow from universal consent that a proposition must originate in reason alone. But, worse than this, he writes, there are no propositions to which all of humankind universally assent. Locke offers two separate but related lines of argument. The first challenges that since children and "idiots" (by which we can take him to mean people who are not in possession of mature reasoning skills) do not recognize these sorts of propositions to be true, it is simply false to say that they are innately known by the mind (if by innately known we mean, in the naïve sense, that the proposition is something of which every mind is conscious from birth). Of course, the position most of Locke's innatist opponents hold does not require that the principles be present to consciousness: though we may not actually have entertained these ideas, they are known, or at least recognizable, by the mind nonetheless. This is held to be the case by thinkers such as More and Stillingfleet, on the grounds that these propositions are so immediately assented to once the mind is presented with them. Locke thinks this is a very weak claim for their innateness, since it boils down to a trivial claim about the capacity of human reason to discover truths. This brings us to Locke's second line of attack. As Locke sees it, if any proposition a person discovers to be true must have been an innate one, the innatist is in danger of implying that a person could reach the end of her life never having discovered a host of truths that were planted in her mind from birth. This would mean that these truths are, at once, in the mind but never conscious to the mind, which Locke considers an untenable position. The innatist will, of course, counter that principles are innate in the sense that they are truths the mind is capable of discovering through the use of reason. Locke argues that this not only fails to prove that these propositions are innate, but, worse, leaves us no way of sorting the innate principles unveiled by the use of reason from all the non-innate principles we discover to be true through the use of reason. There is simply no way, he argues, of sorting out the principles we learn via experience and reason, and those the mind supposedly remembers from its store of innate knowledge. In fact, he points out, the process of discovering the truth of something such as a geometrical theorem could as easily rely on our reasoning about our ideas, and perceiving the relations between them, as upon some immediate assent arising from the recollection of innate principles. If the former is generally our method for the discovery of truths, then how is it that we determine whether a principle of which we discover the truth is an innate one or simply the result of careful reasoning? Thus, he writes,

> I desire to know how first and innate Principles can be tried; or at least it is reasonable to demand the marks and characters, whereby the genuine, innate Principles may be distinguished

from others; that so, amidst the great variety of Pretenders, I may be kept from mistakes. (1.3.27)

Locke begs "a little truce with prejudice and the forbearance of censure" (1.3.28) as he lays out his alternative theory of the origin of speculative and practical principles.

A dominant theme of Locke's discussion is that of epistemic justification—in other words, the reasons one gives for claiming a proposition to be true or false. He begins by pointing out that the principles most commonly taken to be innate are not in fact immune from the demand for justification. Some, he grants, are analytically true, by virtue of definition (e.g. *it is impossible for the same thing to be and not to be*). In such cases, we perceive their truth on the basis of the definition of terms alone. But even in the case of analytically true principles, our assent is not obviously innate; the imputation of innateness ignores the fact that for anyone to see the truth of such propositions, she must first be cognizant of the terms involved and the ideas to which these terms refer. Particularly in the case of the general terms, which are the content, most often, of analytic propositions, people have to learn these terms and their signification and do simply see their relations upon first hearing the words. Locke wonders in what sense this is an innate proposition, as opposed to one that is perceived to be true by a process of reasoning from our learned concepts and vocabulary.

Non-analytic propositions, Locke continues, need to be proven to be true, and are not simply immediately grasped by any rational person who hears them for the first time. Very few people can see the truth of the Pythagorean theorem upon first seeing it, for example. Once it is explained to us, and we follow the steps of the proof, most rational people assent to its truth, but this is an assent that requires a clear understanding and thorough examination of the proof, or what Locke refers to as the demonstration. This does not make demonstrative propositions less true than analytical ones, but their truth is perceived less immediately. The point, however, is that many of the principles held to be innate actually turn out to rest upon rational proofs, which are the reasons one gives one's assent to them as true, and, in the absence of a thorough understanding of the concepts involved, no amount of innateness is going to make their truth clear to the mind.

In considering practical principles, Locke argues that not only is the knowledge of moral rules not universal and uniform across cultures, but even where a set of moral rules are in place and universally assented to, the perception of their truth depends on critical analysis, or, as Locke puts it, on "some exercise of the Mind" (1.3.1). They do not simply lie open to the mind, nor are they immediately assented to upon our first hearing them (which is confirmed by the great number of people who pay them no heed). People assent to moral principles on the basis of reasons given in their defense, and not immediately upon being told they are true. Locke does not deny that many of our most basic moral principles have a reasonableness that a thinking person cannot deny, but this, Locke argues, actually serves the argument against their innateness. If they were imprinted in our minds in some way, they would constantly influence us (and, again, the great numbers of us who have acted against moral dictates from time to time are proof against this). Added to this, considering that there is no way of recognizing innate truths as distinct from rationally derived truths, Locke asks whether it is not a more reliable guide to the truth of moral propositions that we just, as a matter of course, scrutinize our beliefs and subject them to critical analysis. The innatists fail to show why innateness does anything more, or anything better, than analysis and rational deduction by way of providing epistemic justification for the practical and speculative principles we commonly take to be true.

Books I and II of the *Essay* present somewhat different approaches to the issue of innateness and its epistemological relevance. In Book I, Locke presents his arguments against the possibility of innate principles, and in Book II he sets out to show that our ideas are all experiential in origin. Although Locke is clearly evoking a uniform commitment to the view that the content of the mind cannot have its origins in reason itself, these two books have struck some readers as dealing with two different issues. Book I is an explicit argument against innate principles and not against innate ideas. The positive theory of Book II is an account of the experiential origins of ideas, which serve as the building blocks for propositions, but which are not, clearly, propositions themselves. The conclusion that some commentators have drawn is that Book I proves only that propositions are not innate, leaving the doctrine of innate ideas unharmed. In other words, Locke does not seem to have laid the proper groundwork for Book II.

Why, then, does Locke start with the repudiation of innate principles, when his real interest in Book II centers on the experiential origin of innate ideas? Locke's decision to make this his opening salvo is hardly a mistake, considering the multiple editions the *Essay* went through in Locke's lifetime. The more plausible answer is that Book I can be seen as setting the epistemological tone for the *Essay*. Locke is making a case against reason as the sole source of speculative or practical principles. He asserts at the outset of Book I that it would be sufficient to convince those who do not subscribe to the innate principles view that all human knowledge is founded in the natural sensory faculties and not in reason alone. But, he explains, in order to better convince those who are of the opinion that knowledge is founded in innate principles, he will begin by setting out "the Reasons, that made me doubt of that Opinion" (1.2.1). The large project of the *Essay* is not merely an accounting of the origin of ideas, however, but a pointing out of the dangers of overblown opinions that exceed the boundaries of analysis or empirical verification. His introduction to Book I recounts his reason for undertaking the *Essay*. Here he writes as follows:

> I suspected we began at the wrong end, and in vain sought for Satisfaction in a quiet and secure Possession of Truths, that most concern'd us, whilst we let loose our Thoughts into the vast Ocean of *Being*, as if all that boundless Extent, were the natural and undoubted possession of our understandings . . . Thus men, extending their Enquiries beyond their Capacities, and letting their Thoughts wander into those depths, where they can find no sure Footing, 'tis no Wonder, that they raise questions, and multiply Disputes . . . (1.1.7)

Holding general principles to be innate allows thinkers to simply assume their truth rather than make serious steps toward understanding the grounds for believing them to be true. The first step, it seems to Locke, is to show that general principles cannot be innate, and thereby clear the way for a plausible positive account of how these general principles are arrived at by the mind and how their truth or falsity ought best to be determined.

BOOK II: LOCKE'S EMPIRICIST THEORY OF IDEAS

The cornerstone of Locke's epistemology is his theory of ideas, according to which ideas are the basic content of human consciousness. For Locke, ideas are defined as "[w]hatsoever the Mind perceives in it self, or is the immediate object of Perception, Thought, or Understanding" (2.8.8). The project of Book II is to describe the nature and origin of ideas. At the outset, Locke sets the stage for this project with the following proposal: "Let us suppose the Mind to be, as we say, white Paper, void of all Characters, without any *Ideas*: How comes it to be furnished?" (2.1.2). As Locke conceives it, the mind is dispositionally capable of thinking, but it cannot do so until it is furnished with ideas. The mind acquires ideas via two experiential routes: sensation or reflection. Sensation, for Locke, is an "Impression, or Motion, made in some part of the body, as produces some Perception in the Understanding" (2.1.23). Once the mind receives an idea from sensation, it begins considering, reasoning, remembering, believing, and all the other mental operations of which it is capable. By turning its gaze inward, so to speak, the mind also perceives these operations themselves, and thereby, Locke explains, "stores it self with a new set of *Ideas*, which I call *Ideas* of *Reflection*" (2.1.24).

Sensation and reflection are the two exclusive routes by which the mind receives ideas. But precisely what kind of information do we get through these avenues of experience? Locke's theory is best described as compositionalist. While the greatest number of ideas we routinely think about are ideas of things with a multitude of characteristics (such as tree, person, or dog), these are actually complex ideas composed by the mind out of foundational ideas derived from experience. Locke calls these *simple ideas*, which are like atomic entities, in the sense that they are the basic building blocks of all the complex ideas and propositions of which the mind is aware at any given moment. To illustrate the simplicity of experiential ideas, consider the idea of a rose. It may seem to be the singular idea of a particular object, but in fact it is an idea composed from a complexity of simple ideas. If we carefully analyze the idea of a rose, we can actually identify the various simple ideas and their experiential source: the idea of red, which comes from vision; the idea of soft, from touch; the idea of scent, from smell; and so on. Each of these ideas enters the mind as a distinct perception. Locke's account of simple ideas introduces not only the foundations but the limits of human understanding. As he explains at the end of chapter I, the fact that we have five senses means that the information we get about the world is necessarily restricted. If we had four senses and were made without taste buds, then we would never impute the quality of flavor to anything in the world; it would be, so to speak, off our radar. It is possible to imagine beings with six or seven senses, who might have sensory experiences of qualities of things in the world that we will never be aware of. Locke challenges that this is a point anyone who does not "set himself proudly at the top of all things" (2.1.3) should be prepared to accept.

COMPLEX IDEAS

The implication for a compositionalist view such as Locke's is that the complex ideas the mind entertains are *not* ideas directly derived from experience. We never directly perceive the composite rose itself, but only the sense data received piecemeal by our minds. For Locke, all of our complex ideas, like that of a rose, are constructed by the mind from simple ideas. While the mind is "wholly passive" (2.12.1) in the reception of simple ideas, it is very active in building complex ideas, and propositions about them, once it has been furnished with these basic building blocks.

For Locke, complex ideas are ideas either of modes, substances, or relations. The distinction Locke draws between modes and substances is especially important for Locke's theory of ideas. As complex ideas, both are constructed by the mind from simple ideas of sensation or reflection. Both also have what Locke calls real and nominal essences. However, while, in the case of modes, the nominal and real essences are the same, in the case of substances, the real essence is unknown to us.

For Locke, the real essence of a thing is its internal constitution, such that all the qualities of that thing flow from it in a true unity; the nominal essence is the essence imputed to it through the creation of complex ideas. We have knowledge of real essences when we have a complete picture of a thing's intrinsic and necessary properties and how these properties are united. Let us take, as an example, the rather obscure geometrical idea of a chiliagon (a thousand-sided figure). In this case, the idea consists of a combination of simple ideas, combined by the human mind and representing nothing that actually exists in the extra-mental world. The combination of ideas that go into the general idea of a chiliagon is arbitrary, since the idea *chiliagon* itself originated in the human mind. This would count as a complex idea of a mode, on Locke's account. In this case, we have the idea of a chiliagon's real essence—our idea of the chiliagon *is* its real essence, since we constructed the idea of the thing entirely in our minds. In such cases our ideas are, to use Locke's term, *adequate*. That is, *every* property of that thing corresponds to an idea in our minds.

In the case of ideas of substances, on the other hand, the real essence is unknown. Like complex ideas of modes, they are formed by the mind, comprising all the qualities we take to be relevant and necessary to that thing. The difference is that ideas of substances are taken to represent combinations of qualities that have a real unity in the world outside the mind. These ideas are generally combined according to the manner in which the mind repeatedly receives them. If a number of ideas are always received simultaneously, we tend, Locke posits, to suppose that these qualities have some real connection to one another and originate from some common source. In this way, we determine a nominal essence for the thing. We take these things to have a unity of properties that is fashioned by nature. So our complex idea of a rose *seems* like a unitary idea because we take the ideas of which it is composed to have some real unity in nature. However, since we never directly perceive the unifying principle of the rose, there is a key feature to our idea of it that we do not possess—that is, its actual substance, or unifying structure. Substance ideas are therefore termed *inadequate* by Locke, since there are properties of material things for which we have no corresponding ideas (and we have no way, Locke thinks, of ever getting that kind of adequate knowledge about substances). Because of the inadequacy of these ideas, the real and nominal essences come apart where substance ideas are concerned.

IDEAS AND THE VEIL OF PERCEPTION

The standard interpretation of Locke's theory of ideas is referred to as the "representational thesis." According to this view, Locke sees ideas as intermediaries between the extra-mental world and the conscious perceiving mind. We can think of this as a tripartite account of perception: the object, the mind, and the idea of the object created in the mind. On this reading, Locke thinks of ideas as things caused by some extra-mental object and representing that object to the mind in some way. The idea is a kind of mental picture of the worldly object, and it is the idea alone of which the perceiver has immediate awareness. Let us consider the experience of a color. The redness of an apple is caused in the mind by real features of some object in the extra-mental world and the effects of these features on our sensory receptors (in this case, eyes). The perceiver has the idea of red as a result of this causal process, but, importantly, the perceiver sees only the red idea and not the object itself that caused the idea in her mind. The idea of red represents the object, but only indirectly. The consequence is that humans never directly perceive the extra-mental world, but are only ever directly aware of the ideas that stand between the conscious self and the world outside the mind. The ideas stand as a kind of veil or curtain prohibiting access to the world as it exists beyond our perceptions of it. This might seem to raise some considerable problems regarding the accuracy of these ideational representations—if I only ever directly perceive the red color idea created in my mind, then can I ever say with any certainty that it is an accurate representation of the apple itself? The properties of the thing itself are not perceptually accessible to me, only the ideas they produce in my mind, and this makes the verification of the accuracy of my perceptual ideas seemingly impossible.

An alternate interpretation reads Locke's theory of ideas quite differently. It is referred to as the "adverbial" account of Locke's theory of ideas, and, originating with Locke scholar John Yolton, has appealed to a growing number of Locke scholars. This view sheds a somewhat different light on the relationship between the perceiver and the perceived than we get from the representational reading. The adverbial account rejects the view that ideas, for Locke, are things that stand in an intermediary relationship between objects and minds. Instead, ideas are seen as characterizing the *manner* of human perception rather than standing as the *objects* of human consciousness. They are adverbial in the sense they represent the act of perception; ideas *are* perceptions for this account. The intent here is to salvage a more direct account of perceptual awareness from Locke's theory, thereby saving his view from the unpalatable veil of perception problem. The way this account does so is to read Locke's ideas as the expression of the way in which extra-mental objects appear to the mind. So, for example, on the representational account of ideas as objects, the idea of a color is the mental representation of some hidden feature or activity of the object. On the adverbial account, the idea of red that I get from the apple is a function of the way my mind perceives the apple. On this account we could interchange the phrases "I see red" and "I see redly" with no alteration of Locke's meaning. The advantage of the adverbial account is its rejection of the classification of ideas as objects, thus eliminating the somewhat clunky ontological baggage that comes with the representational view. It also manages to capture Locke's heavily conceptual notion of sensory perception. However, its advantage as an epistemological account is not entirely clear for the purposes of appreciating Locke's approach to questions of metaphysics. The question of representation will arise again, particularly in the context of Locke's ideas of primary and secondary qualities, and in his discussion of substance, and in each case we can see Locke's attempt to strictly delineate what can be said about external reality on the basis of the limits of our sensory perceptions. For Locke, the world that lies beyond our perceptual experiences is simply not something about which we can say anything meaningful, because we can have no ideas of this world. Whether we decide to see this as a dangerous route to skepticism or as simply a kind of epistemological prudence depends on how much we want to worry about the possibility that there may be inescapable boundaries to (and quite likely errors in) our understanding of the world outside the mind. That said, the adverbial account does not seem to resolve the veil of ideas problem with regard to the metaphysics of substance.

At this stage, we can let this debate stand. The central point to bear in mind is that the theory of ideas is Locke's attempt to capture something of the conceptual nature of perception—sensory perceptions are a function of bare sensation *and* my conscious experience of that sensation, whether directly as idea-presentations of sensory phenomena or indirectly via resembling ideas in my mind. Lockean ideas are a central feature of human sensory perception, such that sensory perception is, in a very important sense, as much a mental process as it is a physical process. Locke does, however, try to address the so-called veil of ideas problem by sorting sensory ideas into primary and secondary quality ideas.

IDEAS OF PRIMARY QUALITIES

Locke will not commit himself to the real nature of things external to the mind, but there is a lot he thinks we can say about objects on the basis of the power they have to produce certain simple ideas in our minds. The idea of *power*, according to Locke, is the idea of the ability something has to produce ideas in the mind. So, for example, the idea of coldness is taken as a sign of some power, or quality, in that body to produce the idea of coldness in our minds. The problem that arises in Locke's theory, as we have seen, is that we have no way of verifying whether our sensory ideas accurately represent real features of material things. Coldness is a good example of the problem. If my hand is very hot prior to my touching something, then the object will feel colder than if my hand is very cold prior to the experience. The object has not changed in this case, but it produces two different ideas depending on the conditions surrounding the experience. While we can say that there is a power or quality in that body to produce the idea of coldness in us, we cannot say with any certainty that the idea of coldness represents some real feature of the body itself. Do any of our ideas represent real features of bodies in the world? Locke thinks that our ideas of what he terms primary qualities are ideas we can (with a fair amount of confidence) presume to resemble real qualities in bodies.

Primary qualities, as Locke defines them, are real qualities (i.e. powers) in objects, and those qualities are just like the ideas we have of them—these ideas "*are Resemblances* of [bodies], and their Patterns do really exist in the Bodies themselves" (2.8.15). Primary qualities include ideas of solidity, extension, figure, and mobility. Locke's list of primary qualities is consistent with the corpuscularian materialist science that was gaining dominance in Locke's day. On this view, all matter is composed ultimately of tiny bits of matter, called corpuscles (or what we might now call atoms). The movement of these parts, their cohesion, and their relative fluidity all contribute to the overall appearance of that body and account for its effects on the human senses. Perceptual experience is thus a function of the motion of these particles of matter affecting the senses in certain ways. Specifically, the motion of a body's material parts transfers motion to our sensory organs via impact and thereby produce sensory ideas in our minds. As Locke explains it, objects produce ideas in us "manifestly *by impulse*, the only way which we can conceive Bodies operate in" (2.8.11). Locke's metaphysical commitments are never far from the surface. When Locke speaks of primary qualities such as the "Bulk, Texture, and Motion of [a body's] insensible parts" (2.8.10), he is presuming an atomistic account of matter. For Locke, the ideas we have of primary qualities are inseparable from the real object, since they represent the qualities of atoms. Evidence for this is not offered in great detail here, but Locke is not necessarily slipping something past us by failing to account for his corpuscularian (or atomistic) leanings.

Locke admits at the end of chapter VIII that he "engaged in Physical Enquiries a little further than, perhaps, I intended" (2.8.22). Locke does not want to commit himself to theories regarding what may be beyond our perceptual capacities. However, this need not inhibit hypotheses that would best explain the relevant phenomena. Locke's distinction of primary and secondary qualities can be read as an attempt to sort through our ideas of material objects on the basis of their explanatory strength. For Locke, the fact that we have ideas such as solidity and texture, and that they provide a plausible basis for explaining perception, makes the corpuscular picture the best going explanation. The corpuscular account underlying his theory of ideas provides a reasonable basis for determining which of our ideas resemble real qualities of matter and which do not. Locke is correct to state that without this kind of distinction nothing very clear or comprehensible could really be said about ideas—a theory of mental content has to make some attempt to account for the origin and veridicality of the things we think about, and, for Locke, this origin lies in the material composition of objects. Primary qualities provide the basic causal story for all of our ideas about substances. The microparticles of matter provide us with ideas of their intrinsic properties, but their contact with our senses also produce a host of ideas in our minds that are, if you will, by-products of their material and motive properties. These by-products of material motion are what Locke calls secondary quality ideas.

SECONDARY QUALITIES

Secondary qualities also represent powers in objects to produce sensations in us. The ideas we have of secondary qualities, however, do not resemble intrinsic qualities of objects. These include ideas of color, sound, and taste. These ideas are produced in the mind by the motion of material particles acting on the senses, yet the result is apt to mislead us into mistaking appearance for reality. When we have the idea of green produced in us by a leaf, we might well presume that green is a real quality of the object (as when we say, "The leaf is green"). In a sense, it is a real quality in the object, for Locke; however, the real quality is not a green color, but a power in the object to produce an idea of green in the mind. The object, the leaf in this case, is not, in any intrinsic sense, green, but the motions of its material parts can produce that idea in us under the right circumstances. Rubies, on the other hand, have the power, by their different particulate constitution, to produce ideas of red in the perceiver. In this way, Locke challenges the naïve assumption that our sensory impressions directly reflect the natural world. However, his appeal to primary qualities as the causal origin of these ideas is meant to save the theory from falling into complete skepticism. Secondary quality ideas represent real qualities, or powers, in the object, but in an indirect fashion. With primary quality ideas, Locke collapses the distinction between appearance and reality, and offers us some means of grounding secondary ideas, albeit indirectly, in objects themselves.

PERCEPTION AND JUDGMENT

When the mind receives a number of simple ideas simultaneously, it not only relates these ideas, but it makes immediate judgments regarding these relations of ideas. Judgment, for Locke, is a specific kind of assent the mind gives when it takes two ideas to be related by some third idea. For example, when we relate red and sweet with the idea of some unifying substance in which they inhere, we form the complex idea of an apple, which we judge to be an object having real unity. Judgment is a faculty of the mind that allows us to "fill in" the gaps in our knowledge with probable conjecture. Judgments can be discarded, or suspended, when our want of information is too great to confidently assent to the relation of ideas we are considering. When we judge ideas to be related, our judgment turns out to be right only if it actually reflects a real connection between those ideas; it is a false judgment if it turns out we have assented to a relation between what are, in fact, unrelated ideas. Judgments can be hasty or even irrational. Our judgments regarding objects can even, sometimes, distort the perceptual information available to us. Locke considers, by way of example, the visual perception of a gold-colored globe. The idea we get from sight is that of a "flat Circle variously shadow'd" (2.9.8). This is no different in visual content from looking at a painting of a gold-colored globe shaded to give the appearance of three-dimensionality. But, from past experience, we know that convex three-dimensional figures cause ideas of certain patterns of light. Our judgment draws on past experiences and makes similar inferences in visually similar cases. People with vision connect spatial with visual ideas, but since sight ideas can only be those involving impressions made on the eyes, producing two-dimensional patterns of light, any other qualities we impute to an object are the result of our judgment making quick associations between these ideas and our tactual experiences of objects around us. In other words, objects look a certain way to us because they feel a certain way to us as well. The mind is filling in, with its store of related simple ideas, the dimensionality that we do not have immediately presented to us in vision. We are generally unaware of the degree to which our judgments fill in present "gappy" experiences with information from past experiences. Our minds are so quick to relate information from sight to the information gathered repeatedly and habitually from our senses that we are frequently apt to take "that for the Perception of our Sensation, which is an *Idea* formed by our Judgment" (2.9.9). We may think we are *seeing* dimensionality, when in fact we are supplementing visual data with tactile data stored in our memories. What commonly happens, Locke explains, is that we simply fail to notice the multifaceted ideas of sensation that go into making up our frequently quite visual perception of things.

MOLYNEUX'S PROBLEM

One of the most famous and controversial passages in the *Essay* arises at this point in Locke's discussion. A correspondent of Locke's, William Molyneux, proposed the example of a man born blind who knew the difference between cubes and spheres on the basis of touch alone. Molyneux speculates that if a cube and a sphere were placed on a table in the man's room and he were suddenly to regain his sight, the man would not be able to properly identify the objects (formerly known only by touch) on the basis of sight alone. Locke eagerly accepts this analysis, adding that the mind frequently imputes to vision what has actually been received from other senses. If we only ever touched objects then the strictly visual clues would, Locke and Molyneux suggest, be wanting. It is worth noting here that Locke sets a condition on the experiment: he states that the man "at first sight, would not be able with certainty to say, which was the Globe, which the Cube, whilst he only saw them" (2.9.10). The condition here is that the experiment must measure what kind of distinction the man could make between the objects *at first sight*, with no chance to walk around the objects and see them from all sides.

A typical rationalist's response to Locke is provided by the philosopher Gottfried Leibniz, who argues that the newly sighted man would be able to distinguish the two geometrical figures on the basis of sight alone. Leibniz ignores Locke's condition and argues that if the man possessed the sufficient rational concepts of the geometrical qualities of cubes and spheres, he could, on this basis, tell which was which simply by observing their respective properties. While Leibniz grants that the mind is furnished with ideas from sensation, these are only confused ideas; in making an accurate judgment of things, the mind appeals to *a priori* principles such as those in geometry. In other words, reason itself fills in the experiential gaps with its own innate ideas. Some hay has been made of the unfairness of Locke's condition in deliberately stacking the deck in favor of his theory. However, whether the man can look all around the cube or not, the point to be gleaned from Locke's and Leibniz's respective answers is not affected—the question at issue here is whether spatial qualities can be inferred from sight alone. If the answer is yes, then the mind is adding something not given in sensory perception but which it must already have known. Locke's answer is that the only ideas we have are experiential. Since the newly sighted person has no past experience of relations between visual and tactile ideas, he has no ideas of the visual cues that we connect with three-dimensionality with which to make judgments about what he perceives. Sighted people know how angles look because they have both felt them and looked at them, and they have put these ideas together to form judgments in future visual situations. The newly sighted person has no such store of data.

This example sheds light on Locke's theory of perception and judgment. Reason associates ideas and produces a (hopefully) plausible account of the nature of objects. But reason can work only with the ideas it is given in experience. The blind man has no intellectual resources for making the connection between the feel of a sphere and the look of a sphere—not until he has actually both seen and felt one. The issue has undergone a dizzying amount of analysis in light of a variety of experimental considerations. It is not clear that this is an issue that can be easily settled by appeal to case studies or human physiology; experiments even recently have been inconclusive. However, the relevant point for Locke's theory is that the mind cannot simply apply geometrical concepts such as three-dimensionality in some *a priori* manner. The visual cues are not sufficient for this, regardless of how much the newly sighted person might know about geometry. Ideas of figure and dimensionality are acquired over time, with the combined perceptual experiences of touch and sight. The relations we draw between our experiential ideas are formed, and perfected, through repeated perceptual experiences, for Locke.

LOCKE'S ETHICS OF BELIEF

Locke's work can be seen as not merely descriptive but prescriptive as well: Locke seeks to propose a foundation for taking intellectual responsibility for the judgments we make regarding the truth or falsity of ideas. In fact, Locke's theory of ideas is predicated on the notion that our complex ideas and the propositions we build from them are the constructions of the human mind. This leaves us with a great deal of intellectual freedom but at the expense of any innate, traditional, or foundational axioms on which to base our systems of belief. Every rational individual has access to the foundations of knowledge on Locke's account—experiential ideas—and each person is capable of making judgments regarding those ideas in more or less intellectually responsible ways to the end of providing for our needs. As we have seen, Locke thinks we can trace the causal origins of our ideas and sort out those which represent reality and those which do so only indirectly. On these foundations, we can begin to evaluate the relations we draw between our ideas and then alter our judgments accordingly. For Locke, this has more than merely intellectual ramifications. There is a moral tone to Locke's discussion that characterizes it as an ethics of belief—the view that we each have a duty to ensure that our beliefs are rational and well-founded not only for the pursuit of knowledge, but for the broader goods of social harmony, happiness, trust, and mutual respect.

The appeal to tradition and authority did not strike Locke as providing sufficiently rigorous standards for determining the truth or falsity of our beliefs. Without a clear comprehension of the origin of ideas and proper grounds for accounting for the beliefs they hold, people are liable to be the victims of authority and prejudice in the "posture of blind Credulity" (1.4.24). The presumption of innateness has led effectively to an end of critical inquiry, relieving each person of the duty of properly examining the grounds for her beliefs; innateness being once accepted, Locke explains, "it eased the lazy from the pains of search, and stopp'd the enquiry of the doubtful" (1.4.24).

Locke presents the reader with an evidentiary requirement for belief, beyond which we have no excuse for holding beliefs to be true. In Book IV, he explains that anyone must accept this who is motivated by a love of truth. As he writes,

> [w]hoever goes beyond this measure of Assent, 'tis plain receives not Truth in the Love of it; loves not Truth for Truths sake, but for some other bye end. For the evidence that any Proposition is true (except such as are self-evident) lying only in the Proofs a Man has of it, whatsoever degrees of Assent he affords it beyond the degrees of that Evidence, 'tis plain all that surplusage of assurance is owing to some other Affection, and not to the Love of Truth: It being as impossible, that the Love of Truth should carry my Assent above the Evidence, that there is to me, that it is true. (4.19.1)

For Locke, however, this is about more than just intellectual accountability. He speaks, at times, as if we have a *moral* duty to attend to these belief requirements as well. Taking evidentiary limits as one's guide is the means to fulfilling one's duty as a rational being. As he warns,

> He that believes, without having any Reason for believing, may be in love with his own Fancies; but neither seeks Truth as he ought, nor pays the Obedience due to his Maker, who would have him use those discerning Faculties he has given him, to keep him out of Mistake and Errour. (4.17.24)

Reason is a God-given faculty, for Locke, and this is a key element in his ethics of belief. God created each of us with the end of living our lives as well as we can, and employing reason is the surest way to this end. Living according to reason, Locke explains, keeps each person from error and provides the satisfaction of "doing his Duty as a rational Creature" (4.17.24). It is an egalitarian vision of individual self-realization, if you will.

According to Locke scholar Nicholas Wolterstorff,

> Locke's picture of the community of responsible believers is the picture of democracy in which each listens to his or her own inner voice of Reason and no one treats any voice outside himself or herself as authoritative—unless his or her Reason tells him or her to do so.[6]

This makes each of us a better person, and as a result makes society better as well. A society of credulous people is one that is subject to tyranny and abuse. It is no small power, Locke warns, "to have the Authority to be the Dictator of Principles, and Teach of unquestionable Truths; and to make a Man swallow that for an innate Principle, which may serve to his purpose, who teacheth them" (1.4.25). W.K. Clifford echoes this sentiment in his famous essay "The Ethics of Belief," where he writes,

> The danger to society is not merely that it should believe wrong things, though that is great enough; but that it should become credulous, and lose the habit of testing things and inquiring into them; for then it must sink back into savagery.[7]

Locke's *Essay* repeatedly warns readers of the dire effects of irrationality and gullibility. It is a leitmotif of the work that humans are better, and human society happier, when individuals take intellectual responsibility for the beliefs they hold. People who are denied free access to a wide range of opinions about the world, gained through reading and rational inquiry, are, Locke writes, "confined to narrowness of Thought, and enslaved in that which should be the freest part of a Man, their Understandings" (4.20.4). In such states, effort is made by authoritarian Governments to

> propagate Truth, without Knowledge; where Men are forced, at a venture, to be of the Religion of the Country; and must therefore swallow down Opinions, as silly people do Empiricks Pills, without knowing what they are made of, or how they will

work, and have nothing to do, but believe that they will do the Cure. (4.20.4)

We must endeavor to do the best we can as rational beings; however, Locke does not see this as an easy task.

ERROR AND THE ASSOCIATION OF IDEAS

The very nature of human cognition leaves us susceptible to errors in judgment, according to Locke. The reason for this is the continual inclination of the human mind to form connections between ideas. This is something the mind does very quickly, and it does so largely on the basis of habitual and repeated experiences. So, for example, the mind very quickly makes the connection between the perceptual experience of sunlight and the attendant experience of warmth. On the basis of repeated experiences, we come to associate the idea of warmth with the sun, and this goes into making up our complex idea of the sun. Without this natural proclivity of the mind to move from one idea to another related idea, we would be unable to formulate judgments about the world. However, this natural tendency of the mind is a double-edged sword. People, Locke observes, hold all kinds of views that strike us as odd or extravagant. We are very good at pointing to wrong-headed views in others, but are often very bad at recognizing erroneous judgments of our own. Although self-love has some part to play in this, it is not the whole story. Education and prejudice also play some role, but, again, are not the root cause:

> he ought to look a little farther who would trace this sort of Madness to the root it springs from, and so explain it, as to shew whence this flaw has its Original in very sober and rational Minds, and wherein it consists. (2.33.3)

While the mind does a very good job at noting correspondences and connections between our various simple and complex ideas, it does so with a greater or lesser degree of empirical exactness. So, when the mind makes a connection between sunlight and warmth we tend to think of this as being a fairly accurate representation of the sunlight and its qualities. However, if someone were to believe that there is a connection between sunlight and the divine power of a sun deity, we might say that this connection is a more controversial association of ideas that is not strictly reflective of perceptual experience of the sun. This kind of connection seems to be more a product of custom, tradition, and education. Associations can also be made on very idiosyncratic grounds: a person who becomes very ill after eating a certain food may come to associate that food with illness. The very idea of that food will make her think of illness. Again, this is not an association that we might think of as reflective of the powers of that object, but a confused causal connection instead.

Once the mind has made these connections, it is, Locke writes, "very hard to separate them, they always keep in company, the one no sooner at any time comes into the Understanding, but its Associate appears with it" (2.23.5). In much the same way that a musician can play a song perfectly the same every time, owing to the fact that the ideas of the notes are all connected very deeply in her mind, the sun worshipper will make the connection between sunlight and the deity whenever the idea of sunlight is before her mind. People make all kinds of connections between ideas, imputing causal connections between things that are not actually causally connected, or attributing qualities to things that do not, in nature, have such qualities. So, if we consider the range of associations people form, from a belief in witchcraft via the evil eye, to spirits at work in matter, or even that the colors and sounds of objects are directly represented in perception, we see that people are capable of forming associations of ideas on less than purely empirico-rational grounds. The fact that the mind is capable of forging such strong links between ideas accounts for why our mistaken judgments can be taken for truths even by otherwise quite rational people. It is this fact of our cognition, he writes, that "gives Sence to *Jargon*, Demonstration to Absurdities, and Consistency to Nonsense, and is the foundation of the greatest, I had almost said, of all the Errors in the World" (2.33.18). The greatest mistakes happen, Locke thinks, when the mind unites things that are not actually joined. This leads to a host of very serious errors, including prejudice, bad science, and intolerance. Locke's answer is to inspect the grounds for one's associations of ideas, for it is in the fullest comprehension of the origin of our ideas and the proper basis for their connection to one another that we can escape, to whatever degree possible, the confines of prejudicial reasoning.

Locke seems to hold out hope that we can improve our reasoning by thoughtful examination of the grounds for the associations we make between our ideas. In fact, Locke sounds as though this is required for any rational person given the dire consequences of holding ill-founded beliefs based on mistaken associations of ideas. Locke's taxonomy of ideas is intended as groundwork for assessing and analyzing the beliefs one holds. In understanding the source of our ideas, we understand not only the limits of knowledge, but also the proper grounds for evaluating the beliefs we hold. This comes out most clearly in Book IV of the *Essay*, which deals with knowledge and opinion. However, it is hinted at in the final chapter of Book II. We have the means of determining the experiential cause of our ideas, and if we are careful we can sort out the kinds of associations between ideas that have some plausible cause in the real nature of things and those that are confused misapprehensions arising from custom and prejudice. As Locke explains in Book IV, true reasoning consists in finding out the proofs for one's beliefs, ordering those proofs clearly, establishing the connections between them plainly and simply, and drawing the reasonable conclusion from them. The first step in this program is grasping the nature and origin of our ideas, and learning how to sort our ideas out clearly. The way to knowledge is, Locke writes in Book IV, "*to* get and *fix in our minds clear, distinct, and complete* Ideas, as far as they are to be had . . . and by *comparing them with one another*, finding their Agreement, and Disagreement, and their several Relations and Habitudes" (4.12.6). The more care we take in attending to this process, the better we will be at distinguishing truths from falsehoods.

CHAPTER TWO

LOCKE'S THEORY OF MATTER

In Locke's day, the nature of material bodies was an intensely debated and deeply divisive issue. It might seem an odd thing to debate so fiercely; however, in the seventeenth century, the scientific revolution was redefining the most basic conceptions of matter, mind, and universe. Natural science was undergoing a radical shift at the most basic levels. While the traditional Scholastic science followed Aristotle in thinking that the natural world was composed of objects with fixed spiritual essences, the materialistic atomism introduced by modern science posed fundamental challenges to the traditional scientist's core beliefs. Scientists of the new mold embraced a theory of the natural world that influenced thinking about bodies themselves and the relative precision of scientific classification. Locke's adoption of new scientific principles shaped his views regarding not only material substance, but the identity of substances, the classification of natural kinds, and the significance of general terms. For this reason, a thorough understanding of Locke's position requires some familiarity with the significance of the debate over substance in Locke's day.

Many of us are familiar with the term *substance*, which is commonly used to mean "thing," "stuff," or even to denote, metaphorically, some weighty or permanent foundation in a discussion, a person's work, or even a person's character (e.g., a "person of substance"). While this common usage maps onto the philosophical sense of the term, the common notion does not entirely capture the term's philosophical significance. For a philosopher, *substance* typically denotes some basic entity that constitutes things in the world. Substances (e.g., atoms) are the fundamental building blocks of reality, and ultimately account for the actions and appearances of things. A related conception of substance is that of substance as a *substratum*—that is, a *thing* which is the *bearer* or *holder* of properties and which is conceived, in some sense, distinctly from perceivable properties, but which unifies or grounds them in some way. In order to understand this more clearly, consider the claim "The dog has brown fur." The presumption is that there is some *thing having* the quality of brown fur. We commonly make such claims, and in so doing presume that something unites perceivable qualities into one cohesive entity. Despite the fact that anything we say about the dog is going strictly to involve observable properties, most people would be disinclined to assert that the dog, as such, is nothing more than a bundle of perceivable properties cohering in nothing at all.

The existence of substance as an ontological entity, as distinct from the properties a thing exhibits, has long been heavily debated. To assert the existence of substrata risks holding either of two untenable positions: either we are asserting the existence of bare particulars (particular things that have no qualities in themselves, but are the holders of qualities), which are conceptually baffling, or we are proposing the existence of something which is, in principle, concealed from direct perception. In Locke's day it was an idea that many adherents of the new science were beginning to question, though even atomism relied upon an inference from perceivable qualities to their imperceptibly small material causes. But just what is the relationship between the substance and the qualities of objects? Much of what Locke has to say about substance is informed by the atomistic theory of material bodies.

SUBSTANCE AND EARLY-MODERN MATERIALISM

One of Locke's primary influences in this regard was Sir Robert Boyle, an early, and enthusiastic, advocate of the so-called new science. His theory of body, which he termed the *corpuscularian hypothesis*, was the most famous articulation of the new science's atomistic materialism. According to Boyle, all material bodies are composites of ultimately small particles of matter, termed *corpuscles*. The atomic parts have the same material qualities as the larger composite bodies do, namely size, shape, location, solidity, and extension. The specific texture, shape, and other perceivable qualities of compound bodies are explicable with reference to the configuration of their component atomic particles. On Boyle's account, *substance* denotes these atomic particles. As such, the notion of substance cannot easily be construed as a basic entity that holds or unifies properties. Properties of an object are produced by the motion or configuration of its atomic components, and therefore many of the properties that we perceive—such as color, sound, and flavor—are not actually held by the object, but rather are reducible to the motion of the atomic parts. The nature of substance reduces, on this account, to the sizes, shapes, and relative motions of the corpuscles that make up the compound object. As stated earlier, the result of this theory is that much of what one might want to say about the particular identity of objects will ultimately have to reduce to a discussion of corpuscular motion, and much of what one might want to say about natural kinds of things on the basis of shared properties across objects will likewise have to reduce to a discussion of corpuscular motion.

The corpuscularian hypothesis presented a stark contrast with the Scholastic–Aristotelian view of body and substance, which dominated scientific thinking in Locke's time. According to this view, substances are basic entities composed of matter and *form*. On this account, any explanation of the natural world must refer to matter *and* form as fundamental to our causal account of events or things. Matter, as substrate, has no identifiable properties until it is infused with form, which is a kind of spiritual substance. Form plays the most important causal role in this system, giving to matter all the salient characteristics that make an object what it is. It is what gives a material entity its identity and its persistence over time. The form is a general blueprint or plan that provides the foundation upon which a given set of material characteristics can be said to belong to one single entity; most importantly, form defines the essential characteristics of a thing not only as a particular entity, but as it participates in a general category of things. For example, a particular dog arises from the union of a particular lump of matter with the universal form of dog. On this account, in a nutshell, the qualities possessed by a dog, for example four-leggedness, a particular shape, and a particular canine sound and smell, arise from its possessing the form of dog. Thus, our identification of the object as being a dog is a recognition of that thing's essence or form (i.e., the true nature of that thing as it exists independently of human perception); its substantial unity was identified by its prime matter. In this way, the traditional view relied upon general categories, or

the notion of kinds, as a means of explaining the perceivable qualities of particular things; for example, we can assert that a particular
entity has the form of dog since it exhibits the qualities of dogness.

Modern science grew out of an uneasiness with the traditional
appeal to spiritual causes. Causal explanations that relied upon
such occult causes were seen as nothing more than speculative
imaginings. Thinkers such as Francis Bacon insisted on empirical
verifiability as a requirement for scientific explanation, maintaining
that physical events are best explained by physical causes. As Bacon
conceived it, science should explain nature by looking at the things
themselves, instead of appealing to abstract concepts. Spirits are
rejected by Bacon as having no role to play in defining the nature
of material bodies. Atoms, or corpuscles, are basic substances for
modern science, and they are the constituents of larger composite
entities. The latter are explained in all their aspects by reference to
the relative motions of their atomic particles. With the notion of
substance reduced to particulate entities, the concept of substance
as *substratum* is no longer meaningful. Recall that, for the traditional view, substance is conceived as some subsistent entity that
is the holder or bearer of qualities. For modern scientists, nothing
can be said to exist apart from the minutest particles of matter.
The notion of substance as substratum is, at best, a term denoting
the unity of particles in one composite entity. However, since this
is something that eludes perception, many early-modern thinkers,
Locke included, concluded that *substratum* is not a concept that
can be meaningfully employed in scientific explanations of material bodies.

LOCKE THE "UNDER-LABOURER"

Locke's specific interest in this debate involved the intellectual
implications of empiricist science. In the *Essay*, Locke explores the
epistemology of the science of material bodies, seeking to establish clear boundaries to what can meaningfully be said of them,
and what cannot, within the specific constraints of experimental
science. In his *Epistle to the Reader*, Locke modestly portrays his
work as that of "Under-Labourer" to the great "Master-Builders"
of modern science. He claims not to be establishing foundations
for science or advancing scientific principles, but explains that " *'tis
Ambition enough to be employed as an Under-Labourer in clearing*

the Ground a little, and removing some of the Rubbish, that lies in the way to Knowledge" (*Epistle*, 10). The "rubbish" Locke identifies here refers to the vague language and misapplied words that characterized traditional science. Scholastic–Aristotelian science relied upon a number of fundamental concepts, such as *form, prime matter*, and *telos*, all of which were deeply embedded in the spiritual cosmology of Aristotle, and signified the unperceivable spiritual force at work beneath the perceivable qualities of objects. Francis Bacon famously criticized the imprecision of this terminology as referring to nothing; the terms were empty of content because they could not have been acquired by sensory experience. Bacon's prescription for better science centrally involved constructing a scientific language based on the principles of induction from observation and experiment.

Locke's project, which takes its cue from Bacon's initiative, is to explore the degree to which this strictly empirical method limits what can be said about the natural world, but also the promise this new system holds for scientific accountability and precision. In a famous passage from the *Essay*, Locke offers up the following analogy: " 'Tis of great use to the Sailor to know the length of his Line, though he cannot with it fathom the depths of the Ocean" (1.1.6). As Locke, and many others, saw it, traditional science sought to provide absolute answers to the metaphysical questions of existence—what Locke terms the "vast Ocean of *Being*" (1.1.7)—and, in the process, not only exceeded the boundaries of perceptual experience but spent time discussing mysterious entities rather than concentrating on the perceivable world. It is better to know what our limits are, in other words, than to waste time fishing around in hopelessly murky intellectual waters. We see here a central impetus to Locke's painstaking taxonomy of ideas and his account of the origin of words that is built on it. Strongly influenced by mechanical philosophy, Locke aimed to limit scientific claims about the natural world to the perceivable and empirically verifiable.

LOCKE'S CORPUSCULARIAN THEORY OF SUBSTANCE

Locke's account of material substance is found early in the *Essay*, in his discussion of primary qualities. For Locke, primary qualities produce ideas in the mind that actually resemble features of the object and inhere in the body itself. No matter what changes the composite body undergoes, every particle of its matter will always have the qualities of solidity, texture, extension, and mobility. It is important to note how Locke's discussion moves at once from composite objects to their constituent parts, and this is where we begin to see his corpuscularian sympathies at play. For Locke, the most miniscule parts of matter *are* imperceptible, but not in principle, just as a matter of fact. From observation of large parts of matter, and the division of that matter into smaller bits, Locke thinks we can infer that the primary qualities of matter never change, even at the micro level. Consistent with corpuscularian theory, Locke thinks we have good empirical grounds for our claims about the nature of atomic particles. He illustrates this point as follows:

> each part [of matter] has still *Solidity, Extension, Figure* and *Mobility*; divide it again, and it retains still the same qualities; and divide it on, till the parts become insensible, they must retain still each of them all those qualities. For division . . . can never take away either Solidity, Extension, Figure, or Mobility from any Body, but only makes two, or more distinct separate masses of Matter, of that which was but one before. (2.8.9)

Locke goes on to explain that the ideas we have of secondary qualities such as color, heat, or sound are by-products of the texture, bulk, and motion of the microscopic parts of matter. Locke frequently refers to the "insensible parts" of material things in his causal account of ideas. In fact, Locke goes so far as to write that it is "manifest, that there are Bodies, and a good store of Bodies, each whereof is so small, that we cannot by any of our Senses, discover either their bulk, figure, or motion" (2.8.13). He points out that while this may sound like an appeal to unknown causes, we accept that air and water are made of particles that we cannot discern with the naked eye. Why then is it so difficult to accept that the scent of a flower and its color are ideas caused in us by imperceptibly small particles of matter? Though the motions of particles bear little resemblance to the ideas of color and sound, we should bear in mind, Locke argues, that pain bears little resemblance to the knife piercing our flesh, which we readily accept as its cause. And just as we are likely to accept that the pain is not in the knife itself, but rather a function of the way we experience the knife piercing our flesh, we can, he thinks, understand the distinction between qualities that are "real" and in the material thing itself, and those ideas that arise from our peculiar sensory experience of the thing. For Locke, the materialist corpuscularian hypothesis stands as the best going account of the ultimate constitution of material objects, and Locke takes some pains in Book II to make the case for this position. He wants the reader to see that it is a theory consistent with perceptual experience, provided we are careful to sort out primary from secondary quality ideas.

Although the corpuscularian hypothesis is taken by Locke to "go farthest in an intelligible Explication of the Qualities of Bodies" (4.3.16), he is quick to caution the reader that certainty with respect to the real unity, or coherence, of material objects will always elude the human mind. Despite the fact that we can, with some confidence, assert the material composition of objects to be a microscopic version of the macro world, we remain hopelessly ignorant of what he calls the *real constitution* of material objects: "Knowledge in all these Enquiries, reaches very little farther than our Experience" (4.3.14). Limited as we are to experiential ideas, Locke explains, it seems highly unlikely that we will ever be capable of discovering the real connections between the primary qualities of bodies and the secondary qualities that we perceive. Further, we are actually at a loss to establish, with certainty, that any of the qualities we attribute to objects are *necessarily* connected to each another in one unified object. We can make no claims about the real nature of objects insofar as they are unified in some substratum. We can make inferences to this effect, but, he explains, "the highest Probability, amounts not to Certainty; without which there can be no true Knowledge" (4.3.14). While the corpuscular structure of material objects seems well founded in experience, their cohesion remains elusive.

SUBSTRATUM

Locke's discussion of substratum is found primarily in Book II, chapter XXIII, "Our Ideas of Substances." Locke begins by considering the origin of the notion itself, as a function of the piecemeal manner in which the mind receives sensory information. Although it is true, Locke thinks, that our sensory ideas are singular and atomic, the human mind is very quick to draw associations of various kinds between our ideas. In particular, Locke observes, we commonly draw connections between simple ideas when they enter the mind simultaneously. For example, when I look into a corner of the kitchen, I receive a number of simple ideas, seemingly all at once, of white, rectangular, humming, and cold, and this happens every time I look over there. Because of their simultaneity, I tend to presume that the ideas are in some way connected to one another, and that they all originate in some common source. I might say, for example, that there is something in the kitchen that *has* these qualities (which I call a refrigerator). While I may grant that my mind has inferred the connection between these ideas, the presumption that the relations of our ideas map their mind-independent unity is hard to shake. Yet, if we were carefully to consider the notion of substance, as a unifying substrate for the qualities we perceive, it would be clear that it is not an idea at all, in the strict sense of mental content derived from experience, but a "supposition of [we know] not what support of such Qualities, which are capable of producing simple *Ideas* in us" (2.23.2). Since all we have in our minds are the various simple ideas of experience we get from being in the kitchen, what experiential grounds do we have for asserting that these qualities all belong to some subsisting thing? If anyone were to ask us what the thing is in which all these qualities inhere, we would, Locke argues, "have nothing to say, but the solid extended parts" (2.23.2). If asked what the solid extended parts cohere in, then we would, Locke suggests, be stumped. Locke likens this to the case of the Indian philosopher who believes the world to be supported by a giant elephant. When pressed for an account of the elephant's support, he cites a giant tortoise. Eventually, however, the philosopher runs out of answers and claims that the tortoise rests on something "he knows not what" (2.23.2). The Indian philosopher supposes some support must exist, but can only engage in blind speculation rather than clear experiential ideas. In the same way, our common presumptions of unifying substrata for our ideas of material objects are empty, but are psychologically compelling notions nevertheless. We cannot, he explains, think of the various qualities existing "without something to support them" (2.23.2). Recall that, for Locke, the mind associates ideas that seem related. It does this quickly and habitually. Locke seems to be suggesting that the notion of a substratum captures this unifying function of the mind and the attendant sense we have that these complex ideas represent material things with an intrinsic coherence of properties.

As we will see later, Locke takes a particular interest in the cohesion of particles as it bears on the real essence of material things. Substratum seems to signify, for Locke, the inner cohesion of composite objects. As such, the notion plays an important role in our conception of material things as unified objects, despite the fact that it is a notion that is not founded in human experience. The difficulty we encounter with Locke's account of substance lies in the fact that while he accepts the force of the skeptical implication of his empiricist theory of ideas, he seems unwilling to abandon his commonsense beliefs about the world beyond sensory experience. Does Locke see the concept of substratum as a product of human psychology, or does he, perhaps, think that material objects do have unifying substrates that are simply hidden from view?

SKEPTICISM IN LOCKE'S THEORY OF SUBSTANCE

The identity of composite material substance seems to unravel in the face of Locke's empiricism. Locke's empiricist account of substance brought to light some fundamental concerns for empiricism that later thinkers were forced to address. George Berkeley and David Hume famously offered two very different ways of dealing with the empiricist's constraint on our ideas of substance. Both of these thinkers took the empiricist theory of ideas seriously and sought to come to grips with the skeptical undercurrents in Locke's position.

Berkeley's *idealism* attempted to do away with the skeptical implications of Locke's view by eliminating talk of substances altogether, asserting that there simply are no material objects existing independently of the mind. Berkeley's position seems to run counter to commonsense, which is one among several issues critics had with Berkeley's idealism. David Hume's empiricism fully embraces the skeptical implications of Locke's empiricism. Hume asserts that the mind bundles simple ideas together by a number of associative mechanisms, effectively constructing a picture of the world out of what are actually disparate, singular sensory experiences. There are, he famously asserted, no necessary connections between our ideas, and nothing in our experience can give us any sound basis for presuming that such connections actually exist. For Hume, then, material and mental substances are reduced to bundles of singular sensory ideas.

It is useful to consider these two radically different variations on Locke's empiricism when piecing together Locke's own position with respect to the ontology of substance. Both Berkeley and Hume reject the notion of substance as a support for qualities as a vacuous and untenable one on the basis of their empiricist principles. But where does Locke stand? Locke seems to grant an ontological independence to substances, despite the fact that he clearly recognizes the inadequacy of his own theory of ideas to make sense of such a presumption. His distinction of primary from secondary qualities is a clear signal that Locke not only grants an independent existence to matter, but supposes that there are inherent qualities to matter that are independent of human perception. Recall Locke's explanation of primary qualities in chapter VIII, where he writes "the *Ideas of primary Qualities* of Bodies, *are Resemblances* of them, and their Patterns really do exist in the Bodies themselves" (2.8.15). In his discussion of the idea of substance in general, Locke is turning his attention to the support for these qualities—the thing in which they inhere. He asserts that this is something we infer, with insufficient empirical justification. It is something we always suppose, though, as he says "we know not what it is" (2.23.3). What can we take Locke to be committing to at this stage? Locke certainly posits that there are mind-independent qualities, which seem to have some natural unity, but does that amount to any claim about the ontology of substrata? Locke takes aim at theories that grant ontological status to natural kinds, but he sounds at times more agnostic than fully dismissive of the existence of real unities in nature.

NATURAL KINDS AND TRADITIONAL CLASSIFICATION

Locke is sharply critical of the traditional account of substances as having discernible real essences. According to the Scholastic–Aristotelian account, the perceivable qualities of things reveal to us the essences, or forms, that things in the world really have. By comparing and contrasting the perceivable qualities, we are able to construct a taxonomy of natural kinds. On this account, horses are a natural kind, distinct from mules because, as their distinct perceivable features indicate, they have a different essential form. If we compare and contrast correctly, according to the Aristotelian account, we are picking out real kinds of things that have distinct essences. In Book III, Locke takes aim at this view with his own version of the origin of general kind terms. According to Locke, as we have seen, our simple ideas are bundled by the mind into complex ideas, which carry with them the presupposition of some underlying substance that binds them all together. In this sense, the notion of substratum is recast as a kind of psychological adhesive for simple ideas. But what of the claim that our general terms, which refer to sortal ideas, actually do pick out real unities of qualities in the natural world? Locke begins his discussion by stating quite baldly that general terms "belong not to the real existence of Things; but *are the Inventions and Creatures of the Understanding*, made by it for its own use" (3.3.11).

According to Locke, abstract terms are created when we pick out shared qualities of things and construct a new general category that captures those common characteristics. The general term *horse*, for example, points to a category of things that share the qualities of four-leggedness, swiftness, shape, smell, fur, and so on. The qualities make up our idea of the essence of horseness, whereby we denominate particular things by the name *horse* if those things are found to conform to our general idea. Yet these general term ideas signify nothing outside the mind but "a relation, that by the mind of Man is added to [the ideas of many particular things]" (3.3.11). We bundle our ideas of particular things into kinds for the purposes of organizing experiential data and communicating our ideas in daily discourse. These general ideas are what Locke calls *nominal essences*, literally essences in name only. Given that any real constitution of things is in principle unperceivable, it is not possible for us to know with certainty that our definition of gold, for example, captures all the necessary features that make something gold. Further, we have no way of knowing which features of gold are in fact necessary and which are not. But if we limit ourselves to talking about nominal essences, we can, he thinks, achieve a greater degree of understanding of the sensory ideas we have and the grounds upon which we base our general classification of material things. This is the spirit of Hume's approach to substantial unity, and Locke's account, so far, seems to be consistent with this brand of strong empiricism.

Locke clearly does not want to say more than his empiricist principles will allow regarding the real constitution of material objects. His discussion of the substantial (i.e., mind-independent) identity of things amounts largely to a constructivist account based on the association of ideas. He is explicit that the classifications we construct cannot be founded on the real essences of substances. Though we commonly suppose properties of a thing to constitute its essential nature (we will correct someone, for example, who confuses a bush and a tree because we consider our classifications to be based upon a fairly rigid sorting of relative properties of bushes and trees), there are in fact no grounds for assuming that the properties we impute to trees are necessarily connected to one another in some common material source. And yet Locke is not prepared to say that our classification of objects is wholly arbitrary. Our simple ideas arise from "something that does or has existed" (4.4.12). There are real patterns in nature, according to Locke. He does not deny, he states, that "Nature, in the constant production of particular Beings, makes them not always new and various but very much alike and of kin to one another" (3.6.37). Elsewhere, Locke explains that the combinations of our ideas of substances are not arbitrarily combined "without any real pattern they were taken from" (4.4.12). Simple ideas are associated by the mind, but some of our complex ideas, and general sortal terms, seem to be based on a natural coexistence of properties. When constructing ideas of substances, Locke argues, the mind "borrows that Union from Nature" (3.6.29). There is a reason, Locke says, why no one associates a sheep's sound with the shape of a horse, or the color of lead with the weight of gold. We make our complex ideas of substances out of qualities we see constantly conjoined.

Locke repeatedly makes reference to the real constitution of things, which he takes to be the organization and motion of a thing's material parts, insensible to us but causing sensory ideas of the thing in our minds. In fact, Locke often makes reference to the real essence of objects as something that eludes *us* but not God. For Locke, this real constitution of things is the basic source of all the qualities, primary or secondary, that thing has. It contains the key to the relations of these qualities to one another, their necessary connections, and the cohesion of all a thing's parts. The essence of substance seems to refer, for Locke, to the fundamental organizing principle of things. It eludes us, but Locke does not dismiss it as a feature of the natural world. We cannot denominate things by their real essence, he explains, not because there is none, but because we cannot perceive it. No matter how diligently we organize our sensory ideas, this will still be "remote from the true internal Constitution, from which those Qualities flow" (3.6.9). The internal constitution of things is "far from our discovery or comprehension" (3.6.9). In one passage, Locke speculates about how the world might look to someone with microscopial vision. Though his point here concerns the fittingness of our senses to human needs, he makes reference to the discoveries about objects that such a person would be capable of making. With the help of such eyes, he writes, "a Man could penetrate further than ordinary into the secret Composition, and radical Texture of Bodies" (2.23.12). And it is here that Locke seems to part company with Hume. There is a suggestion that substantial unity has an ontological status, for Locke, that Hume roundly rejected as untenable.

The question of the causal dependency of qualities on the substratum is a murky issue, but there are times when Locke seems to be thinking of substratum as that element of a thing which necessitates that it have the qualities it has—that it will move and be solid, and so on. Locke writes of human constitution, for example, as that "from which his Faculties of Moving, Sensation, and Reasoning, and other Powers flow" (3.6.3). For Locke, it is impossible that humans could have access to this deep structure of things, but it is knowledge that God has and " 'tis possible Angels" (3.6.3). This may strike the modern reader as an odd move for Locke to make. However, there is an important metaphysical point in his theological suppositions. In suggesting that the human mind lacks a God's-eye view of the real constitution of substances, Locke is effectively proposing that material substances have real unities in nature.

But does this mean that Locke takes substrata, as ontological entities, to be these unifying principles? Some scholars have suggested that Locke does, and that substratum amounts to the real essence of things, for Locke. Locke is not explicit about the relation he takes perceivable properties to have to substantial unities; that is, it is not obvious that Locke thinks there is a causal relationship between properties of things and their unifying principles. Others have resisted the metaphysical implication of Locke's discussion, on the grounds that Locke's corpuscularianism erects too great a barrier to any claims about unified complex objects.

CRITICAL RESPONSE TO LOCKE'S THEORY OF SUBSTANCE

Several Locke scholars have weighed in on the issue of the ontological status of substrata for Locke. Commentators have wondered how an empiricist like Locke can even hint at an unknowable unifying support for perceivable qualities. Added to this, Locke seems to be entering dangerous waters by suggesting that qualities might have some causal relation to this hidden substrate. Locke certainly believes that the internal corpuscular structure of things is responsible for their primary and secondary qualities. But Locke does not always seem to be talking about corpuscular motions, particularly when he speaks about ideas of substance in general. The *idea* of the latter, if we can term it such, is something that Locke suggests binds qualities together into some coherent whole. The issue regarding Locke's views with respect to substance and essence has been a source of steady controversy. One of Locke's most famous interlocutors was Bishop Edward Stillingfleet, who debated Locke through a series of published letters. Stillingfleet saw Locke's position on substance as wholly dismissive, and charged Locke with eliminating substance altogether from the natural world. In his letters, he claims that Locke's experiential account of the origin of ideas makes it impossible to account for the validity of the idea of substratum. He charges Locke with suggesting that substrata do not exist, effectively eliminating substance as anything other than a meaningless notion. Locke's answer is interesting. He counters by explaining that his account of substance is not as radical as Stillingfleet thinks; he has no intention of rejecting the existence of substrata. His discussion, he claims, concentrates on the origin and content of notions we hold regarding substrata rather than dealing with questions regarding their mind-independent existence. The vague notion we have of substrata is the best that we can hope to attain, he explains, but he is not, he declares, trying to do any drastic recasting of the traditional conception of substance. In fact, he argues, his view is consistent with the traditional view of substratum as a subject of predication. That the relation of ideas could be founded in nothing is repugnant to reason, he explains, and thus substratum is the thing we presumed as a support to these relations. If we take Locke's answer seriously here, substratum is necessary to our conceptions of substances.

But what is substratum for Locke? If it is some existing thing, without qualities of its own, what relation does it bear to the perceivable properties of things? Some readers of the *Essay* have maintained that Locke's notion of substratum is a relational notion, rather than something with ontological status. Jonathan Bennett, for example, reads Locke as using the notion of substance as an account of predication—that is, as a conceptual tool for making claims about properties being properties *of* something. As such, Bennett argues, the concept of substance or *substratum* may have no content, but it serves an important logical role in property instantiation. For Bennett, Locke's account of substance as substratum is adverbial, in the sense that it captures something of the way we conceive our ideas. This is consistent with Locke's account of complex ideas as bundles of simple ideas collected by the mind. Substratum, then, is a way of talking about this bundling process. There is no extra thing, in this interpretation, that unifies the qualities; the mind posits a conceptual unity to properties but there is not ontological inference here at all. On this account, substance is indicative of the way the mind acts on the ideas it receives; in this way, substratum suggests an action of the mind relating to the ideas of properties, when we consider properties as being instantiated or being properties "of" something. *Thing* or *substratum*, then, is not an idea, but an act of combining ideas. This account relieves Locke of the burden of bare particulars. The upshot is that the real existence of substrata is not a point of concern for Locke.

The problem, however, is that Locke spends a great deal of time talking about substances as being not only the causal origin of our ideas, but enjoying a real unity in the mind-independent world. Locke seems to think that the elusiveness of substrata is a function of our perceptual inadequacies, suggesting that there *is* something substantial that exists, outside the mind, to which we cannot have perceptual access. Locke suggests this metaphysical commitment to the existence of substrata in a letter to Stillingfleet, where he writes that despite the obscurity to the mind of the idea of substratum, which Stillingfleet himself acknowledged, this does not amount to a rejection of its real existence. Locke agrees with Stillingfleet's position that it is repugnant to our conceptions of things that qualities could subsist by themselves. The important point that Locke wants to make is that we cannot discern what "the difference of *Certainty* is from a *Repugnancy to our Conceptions*, and from our not being able to conceive." He continues, "I confess, my Lord, I am not acute enough to discern."[1] Thus, where they both agree with respect to the impetus for presuming substrata, and to the degree of lack of clarity of the idea, Locke thinks Stillingfleet has offered no more by way of certainty regarding substratum than he has.

"Therefore," he continues, "it seems to me, that I have laid down the same *Certainty* of the Being of Substance, that your Lordship has done."[2] Though this could be read as dripping with sarcasm, and Bennett certainly takes Locke's meaning this way, there is good reason to think Locke is sincere. His ongoing interest in the challenge for empiricists in explaining the cohesion and unity of composite objects suggests that he saw substrata as having great metaphysical significance, though ultimately unfathomable.

A rival interpretation to Bennett's is found in the work of Michael Ayers, who argues that, for Locke, the notion of substance is coextensive with the notion of real essence. The reason Ayers makes this argument is that Locke describes both substance and real essence as the underlying feature of a thing, unobservable but constituting a foundation for the qualities we do perceive. Locke talks about substance and real essence seemingly interchangeably as obscure and difficult concepts denoting the internal constitution of a thing that makes it a cohesive and ontologically independent entity. Ayers has been criticized for this view on the grounds that Locke is never explicit in the text that these two terms denote the same thing. However, there is good reason to take this view seriously.

In Locke's chapter on the ideas of substances, his discussion focuses largely on the ideas of real essence and internal constitution. In fact, Locke talks about the limits of what we can actually say about the independent nature of material objects, and often expresses this area of obscurity as involving the cohesion of bodies and the relations of their parts. For example, no matter how much we may know about the effect of the pressure of ambient fluid on the movement of particles of matter, we will yet remain ignorant of the "*cause of the cohesion of the solid parts of Matter*" (2.23.24). A body, he explains, is extended if it is a solid whole, but, Locke writes, we will never fully understand the extension of bodies without understanding "wherein consists the union and cohesion of its parts" (2.23.24). The issue of substance, for Locke, may well, therefore, concern the question of unity and relations of ideas. As Locke writes,

> This Essence, from which all these properties flow, when I enquire into it, and search after it, I plainly perceive I cannot discover: the farthest I can go, is only to presume, that it being nothing but Body, its real Essence, or internal Constitution, on

which these Qualities depend, can be nothing but the Figure, Size and Connexion of it solid Parts. (2.31.6)

As Locke elsewhere makes plain, the cohesion of the parts of matter is a "primary and supposed obvious Quality of Body" (2.23.26). In this passage, Locke is refuting the Cartesian claim to certainty regarding the proper essences of body and soul, namely extension and thought. Locke argues that human beings simply cannot have a clear enough idea of the essential features of body to speak with confidence about extension as its essence. Locke goes on at length about cohesion as the basis for our idea of extension. Body, Locke explains, is extended by virtue of the cohesion of its parts; we cannot, he argues, have any clear idea of extension of body without understanding the "union and cohesion of its parts" (2.23.24). And this, he insists, is incomprehensible. Locke's equation of cohesion with the primary qualities of matter, and his obvious nod to Descartes' essentialism, suggest that, for Locke, real essence refers to the necessary connection between qualities—something that is clearly reminiscent of his discussion of substratum as that which unifies or holds the qualities of things. Locke very likely means to retain the traditional conception of substance as an ontologically independent feature of matter that gives material entities their organization as unified things. But he dismantles the traditional use of the concept by positing it as an empirically unverifiable and therefore unknowable feature of the real world. While the Aristotelians appealed to reason to fill in this gap, Locke chooses simply to leave it blank.

Locke's purpose here has puzzled readers. Why have the concept if you are only going to show that it is meaningless or, at least, unknowable? Ayers, for example, has tried to answer this by saying that Locke is laying the groundwork for corpuscular science, and holding this out as something to be determined in the wake of repeated and sophisticated experiments. It is possible, however, that Locke is assessing our ideas of substances in terms of his larger project of assessing the practical limits on human knowledge. Locke's *Essay* can be seen as a process of establishing the relative standards for knowledge and truth, culminating in a very limited but significant assessment of what humans *can* know. In the process, science can learn something about careful hypothesis and the avoidance of grandiose theorizing, and set its sights on attaining the level of knowledge necessary to our existence as material beings. Locke is assessing the length of our line here. It is not intended as a destructive or skeptical argument regarding substance, but merely as a practical one—necessarily agnostic, but not dismissive. We were not intended, he writes, to have the kind of knowledge of substances that God has, because we do not need such knowledge:

> we are fitted well enough with Abilities, to provide for the conveniences of living. But were our Senses alter'd, and made much quicker and acuter, the appearance and outward Scheme of things would have quite another Face to us; and I am apt to think, would be inconsistent with our Being, or at least well-being in this part of the Universe, which we inhabit. (2.23.12)

CHAPTER THREE

LOCKE'S THEORY OF LANGUAGE

Locke's theory of language is found in Book III of the *Essay*, but Locke makes the first reference to his view at the outset of the *Essay*, in his *Epistle to the Reader*. Locke explains that *"[t]he Greatest part of the Questions and Controversies that perplex Mankind [depend] on the doubtful and uncertain use of Words"* (*Epistle*, 13). Locke's concern, as expressed here, regards the precision of language as a key component of effective communication of our ideas. This was a notable feature of new scientific thinking in this period. Many scientific writers believed that a more precise language would rid science of its antiquated and incomprehensible notions. Francis Bacon famously called for accuracy and simplicity in scientific discourse as a remedy to the Aristotelian taxonomy of obscure terminology. Locke's mentor, Sir Robert Boyle, praised the plainness and precision of the language of corpuscularianism. Locke agrees that obscure language leads to vague or ill-formed hypotheses and the generation of endless debate. A key element, for Locke, in the precise use of language is to ensure that the meaning of our words is as explicit and unambiguous as possible.

Locke takes the modern call for scientific exactness and develops a sophisticated account of the origin and meaning of language. Tying language to his empiricist theory of ideas, Locke offers a justificatory basis for a new language for modern scientific discourse. Locke begins with a theory of meaning, according to which words signify only ideas in our minds. *Signification* is Locke's terminology, by which he means that words stand for or represent ideas in the mind. The meaning of a word, then, is a matter of enumerating the ideas it is meant to designate. If we lack the ideas that a given word signifies, then we are using a word of which we have only an imperfect understanding: *"it is not every one, nor perhaps anyone, who is so careful about his Language, as to use no Word, till he views in his Mind the precise determined Idea, which he resolves to make it the sign of"* (*Epistle*, 13). This certainly makes a great deal of sense. One should not, for example, begin theorizing about vulcanology unless one has a proper understanding of the meaning of terms such as magma and pyroclastic flow. If we possess inadequate ideas for these words, our theories will be confusing and unhelpful. The remedy would seem, then, to be sure that the words we use are words for which we possess the requisite concepts.

But Locke's theory of language is more than a cautionary note on the careful use of words. For Locke, confusion arises not merely from the misuse of words, but also from mistaken presumptions regarding their origin and referents. One of the most fascinating and truly modern observations Locke makes is that our words, like our complex ideas, are constructed by the mind from experiential ideas. This is especially significant with respect to abstract general terms. Abstract ideas are particularly important in Locke's theory, not least because the traditional science built its theories around general classificatory terms, which were taken to reveal a real taxonomy of kinds in nature. Locke's constructivist account of abstract ideas has important implications for what one can say about the real referents of our abstract terms. Locke's theory offers a purely pragmatic account of language, according to which our general terms reflect *our* purposes rather than mapping onto extramental referents.

SENSE AND REFERENCE IN LOCKE'S THEORY OF IDEAS

When we talk, we are always talking *about* something. In a broad sense, language is intentional, since it is used by speakers to convey their ideas to others. If not, then we are taken to be talking nonsense, or about nothing at all. Many of the words we use relate to people or things. A linguistic theory generally attempts to account for the meaning of words in terms partly of their referents—that is, the things they are about. However, the reference of terms is a complicated issue in Locke's account. For one thing, for Locke, words refer to ideas. For another, it is difficult to determine just how representational our ideas are. Let us begin by considering the first point. Locke defines the direct referent of words in the following way: "*Words in their primary or immediate Signification, stand for nothing, but the* Ideas *in the Mind of him that uses them*" (3.2.2). Does this mean that words refer to ideas and nothing else? Does *horse*, for example, refer to an idea in our minds or to the animal running in the field? Given the somewhat insular implication of the former, some readers of the *Essay* have concluded that Locke intended signification to indicate the sense or meaning of a word, quite apart from its reference. The problem with this interpretation is its presumption that Locke has some means in his theory of ideas of distinguishing mind-independent referents for our terms, which brings us to the second difficulty. In order to understand the problem with this reading of Locke, we need to look back to his theory of ideas.

The primary difficulty lies in the fact that Locke thinks ideas only imperfectly, and inadequately, represent natural objects. Our complex ideas of substances are bundled by the mind, and patterned after what we believe are real unities of ideas in the extramental world. These ideas are built from simple ideas caused by the motion of particles on our senses, and attempt to capture something of the real qualities of the bundles of atoms in the natural world. Our complex of ideas of modes is another story, as they are ideas bundled voluntarily by the mind, and patterned after no real unities external to the mind. In both cases, Locke argues, complex ideas are created by us, according to unities of ideas we take to be significant. Part of Locke's purpose in Book II is to disabuse us of the presumption that our complex ideas of substances are representational in any reliable sense, and to suggest that even our ideas of primary qualities are probably, but not certainly, representational. The upshot is that our ideas of substances are barely more representational than our ideas of modes—the difference between their amounting to an inadequate and imperfect representation of extra-mental archetypes in the case of substance ideas. The only thing that saves Locke from idealism or complete skepticism is his mechanistic causal account of the origin of sensory ideas, which explains perceptual experience in terms of particulate motion. The ideas we have of substances have a kind of intentionality, therefore, that modal ideas do not. They are intended to capture their extra-mental cause. But there are only limited means of determining just how far our ideas succeed in doing so, for the reason that all we can ever think about are our ideas. Since we are confined, in this sense, to ideas in our minds, it is difficult to fix the representation of our ideas. Given his account of ideas, it is difficult for Locke to establish a robust theory of reference for terms.

Consider the terms *triangle* and *horse*, both of which signify complex ideas in the mind, the one a mode, the other a substance. Since neither of these ideas can be taken to adequately represent extra-mental reality, neither term can easily be taken to *refer* to extra-mental reality. However, the suggestion that a word such as *horse* does not refer to something in the world, but merely refers to the idea itself, seems odd and counterintuitive. It starts to make Locke look like a kind of idealist who identifies no extra-mental feature to linguistic meaning. This has been the source of a great deal of criticism from philosophers of language. The nineteenth-century philosopher John Stuart Mill scoffed at Locke's view, which he took to be saying that words, having only ideas as their referents, are not *about* things at all. Mill countered, "When I say that fire causes heat, do I mean that my idea of fire causes my idea of heat?"[1] Names, Mill insists, are the names of things themselves, not our ideas of them. In fact, Locke makes very clear that we fall into problems when we presume that any of our words signify anything more than ideas in the mind. As Locke writes, "Names must be of a very unsteady and various meaning, if the *Ideas* they stand for, be referred to Standards without us, *that either cannot be known at all, or can be known but imperfectly and uncertainly*" (3.9.12).

This consequence of his view has struck many commentators as a mistake on Locke's part: Locke is seen as confusing sense and reference. Locke does little to sort these two things out in Book III, offering nothing here by way of a causal account of meaning. But, again, we must bear in mind Locke's corpuscular causal account of ideas. In his discussion of language, Locke is almost certainly presuming this causal account of ideas, which relieves him, to some degree, of the burden of causal explanation for our linguistic terms. That said, Locke's account of representation is not straightforward. The degree to which even our primary quality ideas represent actual qualities of objects independent of perception is a matter of probability, but not certainty. For this reason, it is likely Locke had little interest in grounding the meaning of terms in referents apart from the ideas of which they are signs.

CONSTRUCTIVISM AND WORDS

For Locke, language is purely an artifact of human construction and, as such, has a great degree of arbitrariness about it. Language is a means of communicating the private ideas I have in my mind, which are "invisible, and hidden from others." I do this "by a voluntary imposition, whereby such a word is made the arbitrary Mark of such an *Idea*" (3.2.1). For this reason, there is no necessary or natural connection between words and the ideas they signify. This view was intended as a direct attack on the Aristotelian and Platonistic traditions that were current in Locke's day.

According to the Platonist, language is inextricably bound to Forms. Forms are non-spatiotemporal abstract objects that exist independently of minds or particular things. Forms do not exist in the spatiotemporal world, and therefore do not exist as ideas in our minds. We are capable of knowing the forms, but not by way of experience. For the Platonist, language is a key factor in discovering the Forms: with a perfect understanding of words we are able to grasp eternal essences, since there exists, for the Platonist, a natural and necessary relationship between words and things named. Despite their broader theoretical differences with the Platonists, the Aristotelians held a similar view of language as bearing a natural relation to extra-mental reality. On this account, a definition reveals the real essence of the subject. Perfect definitions state fundamental attributes of kinds. On both accounts, language reveals a non-conventional classification of kinds, whether purely abstract ideas, in the Platonic case, or an ordering of kinds in the natural world, as in the case of the Aristotelians.

Locke's account of language takes aim at both of these traditional views. Locke's theory is, for this reason, primarily concerned with general terms and what he takes to be the mistaken view regarding their meaning—that is, that these terms refer to some extra-mental reality. For Locke, language is accorded no special significance in enlightening us to eternal or natural truths. Words have two functions, for Locke, neither of which involves revealing facts about some extra-mental reality, "being either to record their own Thoughts for the Assistance of their own Memory; or as it were, to bring out their *Ideas*, and lay them before the view of others" (3.2.2). If we make the inference from words to the reality of things outside the mind, Locke thinks we are liable to great confusions. The inadequacy of our ideas of substances precludes us from formulating a complete picture of the necessary properties of things. As he explains, "it is a perverting the use of Words, and brings unavoidable Obscurity and Confusion into their Signification, whenever we make them stand for any thing, but those *Ideas* we have in our own Minds" (3.2.5). For Locke, language itself is the use of articulate sounds for the communication of ideas. There may be animals that can mimic articulate sounds, according to Locke, but these sounds can count as language only if they are signs of "internal conceptions" (3.1.2). Language is defined by its purpose, for Locke, and that purpose is social discourse. As Locke writes,

> God having designed Man for a sociable Creature, made him not only with an inclination, and under a necessity to have fellowship with those of his own kind; but furnished him also with Language, which was to be the great Instrument, and common Tye of Society. (3.1.1)

Locke's pragmatic account is predicated upon the privacy of individual thoughts. As Locke explains, each of us has ideas that are hidden from, and invisible to, others. Words are the means by which we make these hidden ideas known to other people, not by any natural connection between sounds and words, but arbitrarily as signs of our own ideas. They have a secondary usefulness, Locke explains, as the means by which we might record and remember our ideas. In the latter case, the words we use can be as idiosyncratic as we like. However, when our words are intended for purposes of communication, we have to establish naming conventions and aim for precision in defining the ideas that terms are meant to signify. Further, words are effective as tools for communication only if two or more people share the ideas that are designated by any given term. For example, if I use the word *tapir*, it will effectively communicate my ideas to you only if you possess the ideas designated by *tapir* as well. If not, my word will have no significance for you. We commonly suppose that some of the ideas we have in our minds are similar to ideas other people possess; this justifies our impulse to use words as a means of communicating our ideas. We presume that others will have a point of reference in their own minds which the terms we use are meant to signify. In fact, for Locke, if someone uses a word, such as *tamaraw*, for which I have no ideas in my mind, the word is a sign of nothing for me. However, I can substitute ideas I possess with the ideas I think another person is trying to convey. If that person explains that a tamaraw is a bovine animal, brown in color, found in the Philippines, I can take tamaraw to designate something like my idea of a brown cow. As a matter of fact, though, tamaraw are actually more like small water buffalo. In this case, then, we will both have very different ideas in mind for the same term. If I consent to give my ideas the same name as other people, it still designates my ideas and not those of someone else if they are to have any meaning for me at all. But, considering the tamaraw example, we can see how prone to error language can be when we fail to ensure that a given word stands for the same ideas in the minds of two or more speakers. The privacy of ideas thus presents inherent difficulties, particularly when it comes to words such as *democracy, truth* or *freedom*, which designate a host of very different ideas in the minds of people who use them.

To illustrate, consider the example of the child for whom the word *gold* has limited significance. *Gold* might refer only to the yellow color idea, since that is the only idea the child might share with other speakers. The word is then taken to signify the color idea the child possesses. As a result, all similarly colored things are identified as *gold* for the child. Another child might have the ideas of weight and solidity as well, and for this child the word *gold* signifies a body that is yellow and heavy. Both use the same word, unaware that it signifies different respective ideas in their minds. Each of these children uses the word to express the ideas she possesses; as a result, both use the word *gold*, but it signifies different ideas for each. Thus, we are able to see not only the degree to which our ideas constrain significance of terms for Locke, but also the inherent hazards of language as the signs of necessarily hidden ideas.

There are two suppositions people tend to make about their words that exacerbate this problem. It might seem an easy fix to teach people the importance of defining the ideas to which their words refer. But, Locke points out, people simply tend to *"suppose their Words to be Marks of the* Ideas *in the Minds also of other Men, with whom they communicate"* (3.2.4). We generally do not ensure that our ideas match those of other people when we speak, but merely assume that the ideas we take to be signified by a word are the same for the person to whom we are speaking. So, to return to an earlier example, when someone tells me that a tamaraw is a bovine animal, I might well take it to signify my idea of a cow, and say, "Oh, okay, I know what you are talking about," and we go on, even though my interlocutor has a quite different idea of bovine, more like that of a small water buffalo, attached to the term *tamaraw.* We are now each signifying different ideas by the same word, and neither of us has bothered to clear that up. Further, it is difficult to know whether my ideas signified by the term *water buffalo* match your ideas, and so on. A second supposition people make is that their words refer not merely to their own ideas, but to things as they really are. As Locke puts it, "they *often suppose their Words to stand also for the reality of Things*" (3.2.5). As noted above, Locke thinks it is serious error in the understanding of language itself, a "perversion" of its purpose, to presume that our ideas stand for anything except the ideas in our minds. Presuming that the words refer to things outside the mind, rather than point to the ideas we have collected under that heading, can lull us into thinking that our words, and the ideas they signify, have some natural connection to things in the world. The problems that arise in this instance are, to some degree, resolvable by gathering as much evidence as we can about things outside the mind. Nevertheless, it is something we need to bear in mind about language in order to avoid, in effect, reifying to an unwarranted degree the complex ideas we construct in our minds. We will return to this issue in the context of Locke's account of classification and abstraction.

PARTICULAR AND GENERAL NAMES

Locke's theory of language begins with an account of singular terms, but moves very quickly to general terms. The reason for this is that Locke thinks singular terms have only a limited context for their use and effectiveness. He writes, "*It is impossible, that every particular Thing should have a distinct peculiar Name*" (3.3.2). Consider, for example, that if I had a particular name for every flower in my garden, or every leaf on my tree, I would soon lose track of the names and would have a difficult time referring to them quickly or easily. Added to this, other people would have an impossible time trying to determine the signification of terms. While it is the case that our ideas of flowers and trees are all particular ideas arising from particular sensory experiences, we do not, in fact, refer to these things in the language of particulars. Our minds naturally draw associations between ideas and relate these ideas on the basis of various relations they seem to have; so instead of multiple particular names for all the things in my yard, I collect them under general terms such as *flower* or *shrub*. It is via a sort of bundling process that we come to have our general-kind terms. These terms not only make reference easier, but also make our terms of reference communicable to other people. Where particular names are useful in the limited context of people who know and share the ideas I have of particular people, or animals, or places, they are useless in broader contexts when I am communicating my ideas to people unfamiliar with my particular surroundings. Consider the example of someone who is speaking to you and mentions *Rex* in the course of the conversation. If you happen to know that that person's dog is named Rex, then the term *Rex* is an effective means of communication, since it raises the same ideas in your mind as are in her mind. However, if you do not know that she has a dog with that particular name, the word will be meaningless to you in that it will raise no clear ideas in your mind, or it will raise ideas that are unlike her own (perhaps I have a brother named Rex, and the name calls the idea of him to mind). However, if she refers instead to her black labrador, those words will very likely call up ideas in your mind that are very similar to her own (if you have ideas of large black dogs in your mind).

General terms are, therefore, necessary if we are to have meaningful exchanges of ideas with other people. General terms are categories that attempt to capture a broader set of identifying features of things. In fact, for Locke, the most important consideration when examining general terms is their fundamental importance in what he refers to as *"the improvement of Knowledge"* (3.2.4). General terms signify the ideas by which we classify things into kinds. In order to understand Locke's position on general terms, we need to consider Locke's account of abstraction in some detail.

Locke's discussion of general, or abstract, terms begins with a telling, and deceptively controversial, statement. He writes, "All things that exist, being Particulars, it may perhaps be thought reasonable, that Words, which out to be conformed to Things, should be so too, I mean in their Signification: but yet we find the quite contrary" (3.3.1). In fact, he observes, general terms are the words we most often employ to communicate our ideas to others. Now, it may not be immediately obvious why Locke's opening statement might incite controversy. However, it is important to bear in mind the Aristotelian position that dominated scientific thinking during this period. On this view, general kinds are real organizing principles at work in the natural world. Locke's claim that all things are fundamentally particular is a clear statement of his commitment to *nominalism*, according to which abstract ideas and the terms that signify them are a feature of the human mind and not real features of the world. Nominalism entails the epistemological view that humans can only ever have particular ideas, for the very reason that all we can ever perceive are particular qualities. Locke's commitment to this view raises some important questions regarding the origin and the role of abstract ideas and terms. Locke does not deny the immense importance of general terms, and for this reason Locke is not willing to deny that humans have abstract ideas and employ general terms to signify them. And yet, for Locke, they are made up, in some sense, from the particular simple ideas we receive from sensation and reflection. However, if all of our ideas are fundamentally particular, then what ideas could abstract terms possibly signify? The nominalist seems committed to the view that abstract terms are basically empty of content (and this is the view that Berkeley takes in response to Locke). There are no general ideas of experience, the argument goes, and so general terms signify nothing at all. Locke's task here is a challenging one, as he is trying to produce an account of abstraction that is consistent with his nominalism but which also preserves some meaningful content for abstract ideas and terms.

For Locke, general ideas are created by considering ideas of particular things in general or abstract ways. We do this by separating, or abstracting, particular ideas from any specific time and place. In this way, he explains, we end up with an idea that is not an idea of any particular existence. Locke elaborates by considering how it is that children come to use general terms. The infant, he explains, acquires basic ideas from her limited surroundings which her mind quickly collects into complex ideas of her mother or her nurse, and her terms *mother* and *nurse* uniquely signify ideas of her own mother or nurse in the limited context of her own home. With broader experience, the child learns that there are numerous individuals who share with her mother or nurse a general shape, occupation, and other qualities. There are women and mothers and nurses who are like her own. In this way, the child is able to broaden her conception of *mother*, so that the term signifies not only her own mother, but mothers in general, who are women with children that they care for in similar ways. Now, it is important to bear in mind that for an empiricist like Locke, abstract ideas have no experiential content: we cannot have direct perceptual experiences of abstract ideas. His answer to this is that when the child comes to have a general name and general idea, she has not created a new idea, but has merely left out certain ideas of qualities peculiar to her mother Jane or her nurse Mary. She brackets off "that which is peculiar to each, and retain[s] only what is common to all" (3.3.7). Depending on what we choose to focus on, we come up with a host of general ideas. If we focus only on shape, for example, then we might come up with ideas of man and woman; if we focus instead on different characteristics men and women more generally share with other things, we might come up with the idea of animal or of living being. So, for Locke, abstract ideas are still concocted from particular ideas gained from experience. In this way, Locke is attempting to explain abstraction without suggesting that the mind can have ideas that are not derived from experience. As he says himself, if anyone suggests that abstract ideas come from any other source than our particular experiential ideas, they will "be at a loss where to find them" (3.3.9).

When we speak of a thing's essence, what we are really referring to, Locke explains, is the somewhat arbitrarily constructed abstract idea we have of that thing's kind. Recall the example of the two children's ideas of *gold*. Each child uses the general term to signify the ideas she possesses, and those ideas are different for each. Further, their ideas of gold will include certain ideas they take to be important and will exclude others. The essence of a thing is of strictly classificatory use, involving a number of qualities we take to be essential to that kind. The tree in my backyard is the large thing with many low-hanging branches that provides shade on a sunny day; these ideas, and likely more, go into my idea of that particular thing. But what *kind* of thing it is, an oak or an elm, depends on whether it has the properties we take to be salient to our abstract conceptions of the kinds *oak* or *elm* (of which shadiness and low-hanging branchiness may or may not be a part). Locke states this point nicely with his example of the classification of bats. The question of whether a particular flying animal is a bird or some other kind of thing is not a question of "whether a Bat be another Thing than indeed it is, or have other Qualities than indeed it has, for that would be extremely absurd to doubt of" (3.11.7). While it goes without saying that the bat itself has the qualities essential to its particular existence, the question of whether it falls under the general category *bird* depends on what qualities we deem essential to birds and to bats and what we do not. Locke's account of general ideas is thereby strictly constructivist: they are created when we pay selective attention to our complex ideas of things. If we appreciate the way in which general ideas are constructed, then our disputes regarding categorization will be greatly reduced. As Locke puts it, disputes over categorization are "meerly [sic] verbal, and about the Signification of Words" (3.11.7). Whether a bat has properties we take to be essential to it boils down to a question of which ideas we are going to take the word *bat* to signify. It follows, Locke explains, that the essence of a species is "the Workmanship of the Understanding, since it is the Understanding that abstracts and makes those general *Ideas*" (3.3.12).

Does this mean there are no real unities or kinds in nature to which our general terms can be taken to refer? Locke grants that there are, on the face of it, different things in the world which have perceivably distinct features. But the conceptual distinctions we make between kinds are based on incomplete information about the real constitution of things. Recall that, for Locke, the question of the micro-constitution of things is a difficult one to answer. At their very basic level, material objects are all composed of atomic particles. If this is the case, then our distinctions of things into kinds run at a fairly superficial level. These categories are, as such, arbitrary, revealing the qualities we take to be significant, or essential, to a thing and those we do not. For this reason, the essences we actually speak about are *nominal*, since they are essences as defined by the human mind. Real essences of things, on the other hand, are elusive, and, as such, we cannot know whether we are referring to them with our sortal categories. Locke finds this particularly clear in the case of genetic abnormalities. If a horse is born with three legs, or with no mane, then the question of whether it still falls into the category of horse or warrants a new species designation is entirely up to us. General terms generate a confusion, according to Locke, of which we need to be cognizant. Particular things are classified as kinds because we have settled on a category into which they can be slotted. A mule and a horse are different kinds of things, for example, because each has qualities that agree with the different abstract ideas we have generated. It is possible we could have decided on a broader definition of the category of horse such that it included short, stocky, gray animals with a variety of other characteristics that we would not consider salient to its horseness. The vagaries of categorization obviously have no effect on the real essence of the things as they exist outside the mind; an individual mule is still what it is regardless of what *kind* of thing we take it to be. To presume that our general terms actually inform us about the real nature of substances is a mistake. As Locke writes, "A blind Man may as soon sort Things by their Colours, and he that has lost his Smell, as well distinguish a Lily and a Rose by their Odors, as by those internal constitutions which he knows not" (3.6.9). To return to our earlier question, Locke thinks our abstract ideas of substances are attempts to represent patterns we observe in nature. We do not, generally, unite qualities in a totally random way, but attempt to construct ideas that in some way reflect the natural world. So no one would likely include rationality, for example, in their designation of the word *tree*. That said, though we do borrow from what we perceive in nature, *"the number* [of ideas] it combines, *depends upon the various Care, Industry, or Fancy of him that makes it"* (3.6.29). We focus on some qualities and leave out others in the construction of general kinds, and our general terms signify the ideas we produce in this fashion.

REMEDIES FOR THE IMPERFECTION OF LANGUAGE

The first step in avoiding linguistic errors is to understand, as Locke has tried to show us in Book III, that words strictly signify ideas in the mind. The meaning of words, therefore, relies upon the ideas that any speaker and her interlocutor have in their respective minds. This is never simple, however, and Locke explains that there are many words we use commonly—such as names of mixed modes and names of substances—that signify either very abstract and complicated ideas having an external standard (e.g., *truth* or *justice*) or that refer to things outside the mind for which we actually have no experiential ideas at all (e.g., *form* or *substratum*). The correct and careful use of language has both civil and philosophical implication. Language is the means by which we communicate our thoughts and have civil relationships with other people, which would be greatly impeded by lack of clarity and misunderstanding.

Further, however, precision in the use, especially, of our general terms is essential for what Locke calls *philosophical* ends, by which he means scientific and moral knowledge.

According to Locke, then, each person should be careful to avoid the use of words for which she has no corresponding ideas. In this way, we avoid using meaningless words for which no one *can* have experiential ideas. The result is that such ideas will cease to make their way into discourse. In this way, Locke's empiricist theory of ideas can be seen as setting out the justification for a new scientific discourse, as envisioned by Bacon and Boyle, one that is made meaningful and coherent by referring to experiential ideas alone. To this end, we must also seek to avoid idiosyncratic usage and aim to use words as a means of raising shared ideas in the minds of others. It is each person's responsibility to ensure that she understands the signification of her own words properly, as well as that of the words of other speakers. While Locke's theory certainly makes room for individuals going through life with a completely private and idiosyncratic language, he ultimately sees language as a tool for social commerce and the advancement of human knowledge. To these ends, if we agree that these are valuable goals, we bear a duty to make our language clear to others. Given the fact that we have only mediated access to the ideas in others' minds through discourse, the communication of our ideas to others is, while imperfect, to be undertaken with a great degree of care.

CHAPTER FOUR

LOCKE'S THEORY OF IDENTITY

Locke's account of identity, especially of personal identity, has been enormously influential and has been a touchstone for identity theory since the publication of the *Essay*. Locke's discussion is found primarily in Book II of the *Essay*, chapter XXVII. Here Locke begins with a general account of the origin of the idea of identity, and the identification of substances, and then moves on to a discussion of personal identity. Locke's theory is predicated upon the dismantling of the traditional equation of identity with essence, taking aim at the two dominant theories of his day: the Scholastic–Aristotelian and the Cartesian accounts. On the traditional Scholastic–Aristotelian view, the identity of objects or persons depends on the existence of an unchanging substratum underlying the qualities of a thing or person. Substratum coupled with form give things their material unity, and provides the causal basis for their identity. The identity of things or persons, on this view, is continuous and necessary as long as matter and form are united.

Descartes held the essence of body and mind to be, respectively, extension and thought. The identity of objects and selves depends upon the absoluteness and permanence of their essential natures. Individuation of things, for Descartes, is modal and therefore only phenomenal—distinct objects are, in fact, variations of extension. In this way, for Descartes, things retain their fixed and essential nature through change.

Locke's interest in identity seems more psychological than metaphysical, primarily for the reason that Locke's theory of identity is strongly influenced by his corpuscularian views. For the corpuscularian all physical things are reduced to the motion and cohesion of particulate matter, so Locke cannot appeal to a form that fixes the identity of a substance. Though Locke does suggest in his account of substances that they likely have some internal organizing principle, the complete obscurity of such a notion precludes it from forming the basis for our ascriptions of identity. Owing to the implications of this corpuscular view, identity is not as clear and straightforward for Locke as for the Scholastic or Cartesian accounts, and it is also for this reason that Locke ultimately steers clear of metaphysics in his discussion of identity. Locke concentrates his discussion on ideas, concluding, not unlike the essentialists, that the identity of things depends very much on categorization—except that, for Locke, identity is based on categories we construct.

INDIVIDUATION AND IDENTITY

Though Locke's main discussion of identity is found in Book II, Locke makes his first mention of the topic in Book I, in the context of his discussion of innate ideas. Here Locke argues that identity is not an innate idea, asserting that "it will be found, that many grown Men want [it]" (1.4.3). Locke argues that the problems of identity are simply too difficult and persistent for the ideas of identity to be innate. If the concept were innate, he argues, surely we would have a ready and clear answer to the problems raised by continuity of personal identity across changes in physical states, for example. We would know whether a person's identity resides in her soul or her body, or a combination of both. As Locke writes, "our *Idea of sameness*, is *not* so settled and clear, as to deserve to be thought *innate* in us" (1.4.4).

According to Locke, identity is an idea we form when "considering any thing as existing at any determin'd time and place, [and] we compare it with it self existing at another time" (2.27.1). The idea of identity does not involve, therefore, the idea of comparing any idea of an object with itself at any single moment in time. In this way, Locke moves the discussion away from absolute conceptions of identity, such as we find in the Scholastic and Cartesian accounts. These accounts held that identity was determined on the basis of considering an object in itself as having a defined essence; identity over time is thus assured, if we take essences to be eternal. Locke rejects this approach in specifying that an entity considered by itself, in the present, will not provide any notion of its identity, but only of its present existence as a distinct thing. Identity, for Locke, is a matter not of defining essences, but of determining continued existence over time. If we had no sense of past or future, but only of the present moment, we could not possess the concept of identity, though we would be able to individuate distinct objects on the basis of their spatiotemporal diversity. The issue of individuation itself is not of great concern to Locke, as he spends little time developing this concept. However, individuation was a problem for thinkers who held that universals were real. In a world of universals, the individuation of particular things is a matter that requires some explaining. Alternatively, Locke subscribed to *nominalism*, the view that reality consists only of particular objects.

In order to clarify Locke's distinction between identity and individuation, consider the following example: my current idea of the chair existing as a distinct object in my living room is not an idea of identity, but an idea of individuation. My grounds for asserting its distinct existence are simply my perception of its unique spatiotemporal location. It is a mass of atoms configured in a way that makes it distinct from other such masses in the room (myself included). Locke's account of individuation is summed up as follows:

the one thing cannot have two beginnings of Existence, nor two things one beginning, it being impossible for two things of the same kind, to be or exist in the same instant, in the very same place; or one and the same thing in different places. (2.27.1)

Locke thinks this is something basic to our perception of objects. As he puts it, when we perceive a distinct object, "we are sure, (be it what it will) that it is that very thing, and not another, which at that time exists in another place" (2.27.1). Individuation does have an important role to play in Locke's account of identity, however. For something to exist means that it exists as something with identifiable qualities. In fixing a thing's identity over time, we must first be able to distinguish it as the thing it is at any particular moment; identity criteria then become relevant when we think about whether that thing has retained what we take to be its salient qualities from one moment to the next. Individuation works as a kind of snapshot; it is our benchmark for establishing the thing's identity. For example, in reference to an atomic body, Locke explains that it is "at that instant, what it is, and nothing else . . . and must continue, as long as its Existence is continued: for so long it will be the same and no other" (2.27.3). So an atom, existing at any given moment, is identical with itself, but for it to maintain its identity over time, it must retain the qualities we take to be essential to its existence as that thing. However, it is important to note that the defining features of a thing have a lot more to do with our general categories of things than this one example suggests. The atom has features as an extended inert mass that it must retain to remain the same thing. This sounds straightforward—a thing needs to maintain its qualities over time for it to have an identity. But consider a human being. There are qualities it has that are not merely physical. A human being does not remain the same if the being dies. A human and a corpse are importantly different things for us, despite sharing the same physical organization of parts, and the continued identity of the human is not something we take to be based on its strictly physical composition. So, to return to the snapshot moment when we are made aware of an object's individual existence at a particular moment, it is "what it is"—but the notion of what it is has a lot to do with the *kind* of thing we take it to be. Locke agrees with the essentialist views insofar as they hold that identity is contingent upon our sortal concepts, but these sortal concepts are fluid, for Locke, to a degree that neither the Scholastic nor the Cartesian could tolerate. General classifications result from our selective attention to qualities of things; they reflect, in some degree, the qualities things actually seem to possess, but to a greater degree general terms reflect our selective attention to qualities. The question of a thing's identity is determined with reference to our constructed sortal concepts and the collection of qualities we have determined necessary to our definition of a given thing's nominal essence. It is only through these sortal concepts that we have some standard to which to appeal in determining whether we consider the object to be the same object as it was at some earlier time. If I take the shape and size of the object in the living room to be essential to its being a chair, then my assessment of its continuous identity over time will involve its maintaining its material integrity. If it has lost an arm in the intervening time, then I will say that it is not the same chair. My cat, on the other hand, might lose its eyesight overnight, but this will not affect my judgment of its continued identity, since it is still the same living animal, just one that can no longer see. Our judgments regarding identity, therefore, will depend upon the criteria we select as salient to that thing's being what it is.

THE CONDITIONS FOR IDENTITY

Locke identifies three broad categories of things, based on their broadly distinct sets of defining features: inert bodies, living beings, and persons. For Locke, material objects such as rocks are importantly different, for us, from living things such as trees. In this case, then, the identity conditions will be different for rocks and trees. What makes a present rock identical with itself at some previous time or place is the continuity of its material composition: it is a mass of particles joined together to form one thing. But if we take a big hammer and pound it, the rock ceases to have the same material composition it had before. It ceases to exist as that thing. It is no longer the same rock, but a bunch of smaller rocks or pebbles. Locke thereby establishes the identity of material substances strictly in terms of their material composition, and this criterion holds for atoms, for small collections of atoms, and for very complex collections of atoms. As Locke writes,

> if two or more Atoms be joined together into the same Mass, every one of those Atoms will be the same, by the foregoing Rule: And whilst they exist united together, the Mass, consisting of the same Atoms, must be the same Mass, or the same Body, let the parts be never so differently jumbled. (2.27.3)

But if any of these atoms is removed, or another added, then it is no longer the same mass. There is no criterion other than atomic composition that determines the continued identity of any inert physical body, and this criterion reflects the qualities we have taken to be essential to matter in forming the category of physical substance.

Living things have different identity conditions, for Locke. Using the example of an oak tree, Locke explains that the material composition of living things is not as central to their identity as the functional organization of their material parts. The difference, Locke explains, is that inert masses of matter are nothing but the cohesion of particles of matter, while a thing such as a plant or animal has a living principle that constitutes the organization of its material parts to the end of maintaining the life of that thing. In this case, identity is based on a different criterion, reflecting the characteristics we take to be salient in distinguishing living from inert bodies. A plant or animal is one continuous thing if it partakes of the same uninterrupted life over time. This organization of parts, Locke explains,

> being at any one instant in any one Collection of *Matter*, is in that particular concrete distinguished from all other, and is that individual life, which existing constantly from that moment both forwards and backwards in the same continuity of insensibly organized Parts united to the living Body of the Plant. (2.27.4)

In its organization of parts, as a collection of matter, it is individuated from other parts of matter and has its identity as such if that material organization remains the same over time, but its continued identity as a living thing requires a functional organization which "is fit to convey that Common Life to all the Parts so united" (2.27.4). Regardless of whether the oak tree is a sapling or a fully grown tree, whether it loses leaves or branches, if it retains the functional organization of its parts, it maintains its identity.

Insofar as humans are animals, according to Locke, the identity of a human being answers to the same conditions as the identity of other living things. Locke distinguishes between human and personal identity on the basis of the very different criteria upon which each relies, "it being one thing to be the same *Substance*, another the same *Man*, and a third the same *Person*" (2.27.7). In making these distinctions, Locke argues, we avoid unnecessary confusions, particularly with regard to personal identity. According to Locke, a *human* has a continuous identity insofar as the physical particles constituting the body at any given moment are organized under one continuous living principle. As Locke claims, the identity of humans consists in "nothing but a participation in the same life, by constantly fleeting Particles of Matter, in succession vitally united to the same organized Body" (2.27.6). If our identity as continuous human beings were not tied to physical unity, then it would be impossible, he argues, to assert the identity of any human as a single physically unique being; for example, we would be unable to claim that John at age twenty-five is the same being as John was at the age of six. Human identity is not tied to rationality, for Locke, as it was for so many thinkers in his day. Any living being that has a general shape and make like our own is considered a human being, regardless of whether it can reason. No matter how intelligent a pig may be, Locke explains, or how much it may remind us of the

Roman sun god Heliogabalus, we would still call that animal a pig rather than a man or Heliogabalus. Likewise, a rational-sounding parrot will still be a parrot and not a human, no matter how well it converses with others. Locke concludes that human identity cannot be tied to rationality, but to the physical body, with a specific shape and a continuous functional organization of its parts. In fact, it is most likely that coming across enough cases of rational parrots would induce us to create a new sortal category for a rational non-human, rather than including them in the category of human beings, so resistant are we to deeming human anything shaped so differently from ourselves.

Locke's theory of identity is meant to capture the categories we construct and employ in categorizing ourselves and things in the world. Inanimate objects are different from living things according to the general ideas we commonly have of these things. Humans distinguish themselves from other animals on the basis of specificities of physical appearance—again, according to our selective general categories. But there is a further category that carries separate identity conditions, and that is the identity of *persons*.

PERSONAL IDENTITY

Personal identity, which captures whatever we might mean by *self*, *soul*, or *person*, is a distinct category of identity, for Locke, the conditions for which include the ideas of thinking, reflection, and, most importantly, consciousness of oneself as "the same thinking thing in different times and places" (2.27.9). It is in the awareness of one's thoughts and perceptions—an awareness, importantly, that the individual considers unique to herself—that personal identity is founded. This identity extends as far back as that individual can recall past experiences or thoughts of which she was conscious. Identity of persons is therefore established independently of the functional organization of bodies. Why would Locke propose this special category of personal, as opposed to human, identity? Pinning personal identity on shared memory with selves in times past is going to raise some important problems. For one thing, it makes identity "gappy"—since no one has a perfect memory, there are many thoughts and experiences that have been forgotten in any person's life. Do we lose our identity in those moments lost to memory? If I cannot, for example, recall having said something to someone, must I accept that it was effectively another person who said it? This makes it difficult to establish that I am the same person as the six-year-old with whom I share a functional organization, but whose experiences I can barely recall. Added to this, there are large portions of our lives in which we are not conscious. Does this mean we cease to exist when we are sleeping or otherwise unconscious?

To return, then, to the original question posed above—why would Locke have proposed this account of personal identity? Locke acknowledges that this account will "look strange to some readers" (2.27.27). Surely our physical body is constitutive, with our minds, of our sense of self. For Locke, though, the thoughts each person has uniquely define that person in an important way that her physical body does not. The distinction does not contribute to any conception of consciousness as such, however, but rather to our sense of what it means for someone to be the author of her thoughts and actions. Thus, Locke is not suggesting an essentialist distinction of minds and bodies; the intimation of mind–body dualism here is tempered by Locke's empiricist restraint on appeals to essences. We cannot pronounce with any certainty regarding the essential nature of the soul, or thinking substance. Descartes famously proposed that the soul is in essence a thinking thing. But Locke considers this a hasty and unfounded claim. What we can say about the self is based on the empirical evidence provided by conscious experience of thoughts at any given time. The continuity of identity of persons, then, is the awareness of thoughts in the present time, and memories of similar conscious experiences in past times and places. Though the account of self, or soul, ends up patchy, it is, Locke says, perfectly sufficient for capturing what we actually mean when we speak about our identity as thinking, rational selves. The identity of the *person*, therefore, is not to be confused with the identity of thinking substance. This is something Descartes took great pains to establish, but it is quickly dismissed by Locke as being an issue that, in the case of personal identity, "matters not at all" (2.27.10). To tie the identity of the self to issues regarding the identity of the soul, or thinking substance, not only takes us into mysterious territory, but actually moves us away from what Locke thinks we normally mean by the term.

The theory does look "strange" to us, nevertheless. In addition to the metaphysical problems regarding the gappyness of personal identity, there also arises the possibility that multiple persons could inhabit a single physical body. But Locke is actually not particularly worried about these issues. There are, he admits, many moments of our lives that are lost to memory and no one ever has the whole history of their thoughts and experiences present to her mind. For Locke, the worry about gappyness "concerns not *personal Identity*" (2.27.10). But what is it that Locke is setting out to do by defining personal identity, if not to define the spirit or essence of selfhood? Given his empiricist rejection of essences, we might think the notion of selfhood is, as such, something merely to dismiss.

This account seeks to do something other than identify consciousness *per se*—Locke's motivation in singling out personhood is an attempt to capture, and analyze, the way we actually think about moral responsibility. The relevant concern for explorations of personal identity, according to Locke, is the discovery of the relation of present self to past self that makes those past actions and experiences one's own. Locke thus has a specific purpose in bracketing personal identity in the way he does. The key feature of personal identity, for Locke, is personal accountability—the thoughts I have now and have had in the past are importantly mine. The person "attributes to it *self*, and owns all the Actions of that thing, as its own, as far as that consciousness reaches and no farther" (2.27.27). Ownership implies responsibility, and it is in this way that *personal* identity implies moral responsibility. On the one hand, this is a theological issue, concerned with questions of moral responsibility after the death of the body. However, the appeal of this account is not strictly in its theological implications. *Person* is, as Locke puts it, "a Forensick term" (2.27.26), designating a self that is concerned with her own well-being and acting consciously to that end. The thoughts, intentions, and beliefs a person is conscious of having are hers, and as such she is answerable for them.

To appreciate Locke's forensic distinction of human and personal identity, let us consider his example of the prince and the cobbler. Locke proposes the case of a prince whose soul inhabits the body of a cobbler. This is the prince's person since it carries the consciousness of the prince's past life; in other words, it is the collection of all the prince's memories. What would we say about the cobbler and the prince in this case? Well, Locke answers, all who knew the cobbler would say that, on the basis of physical appearance, it is the same man. But, Locke points out, the *man* and the *person* are not the same thing—if we think about it, this is the person of the prince, and regardless of physical appearance, still the same prince who is responsible for all that he has done in the past. To extend the example, consider how we might think about this if the prince were, at the time of his physical transformation, being tried for the murder of one of his servants. The same person remains responsible for the act he is conscious of having done, owns the act, and carries the blame even if he inhabits the cobbler's physical body. Though the prince's body changes, his consciousness remains unchanged. The identity of person is the identity of consciousness, and whatever is not part of my consciousness is not part of my personal identity. If what I do when sleeping ("I" here referring to the same physical human) is not part of my waking consciousness, then it is not an act for which I, as a morally significant person, am responsible—it may as well be another person who did it. As Locke famously puts it, "to punish *Socrates* waking for what sleeping *Socrates* thought, and waking *Socrates* was never conscious of, would be no more of Right, than to punish one Twin for what his brother twin did, whereof he knew nothing" (2.27.19). Locke is trying to capture an important distinction here—physical continuity allows us to say that Socrates has a continuous physical identity with his sleeping self, with his younger self and with his unconscious self, but moral responsibility relies on a notion of identity that is more strictly mental. This is a powerful insight, but one that is not outside the realm of commonsense. Consider, for example, the different conceptions of identity at work in cases of split personalities. Mary is certainly the same human being today that she was five years ago, but if she experienced a severe trauma and suffers amnesia regarding certain events over the past five years, we tend to think she has become a different person. If she regains her memory of the time prior to this traumatic amnesia, would we hold her responsible for a criminal act committed in that traumatically induced state? Crimes of passion, a more commonplace example, are tried on the assumption that the person was not in her right state of mind. In this case, we are relying on a notion of identity that involves continuity of consciousness. Similarly, if a sleepwalker hurts someone while asleep, we may not hold that person responsible when she awakes. These cases involve people who, in some important sense, do not own these acts. Locke's point, then, is to bracket off personal identity as an important moral category involving conscious, responsible decision-making.

CRITICAL RESPONSE TO LOCKE'S ACCOUNT

(a) The memory defense: Molyneux's drunken criminal

On Locke's account, the conditions for personal identity require first-person consciousness of actions as being one's own. At the outset, this may strike many readers as a somewhat problematic account, since it implies that an individual is responsible only for the things she remembers doing. If so, then one is not responsible for the things one does not remember, or at least for the things one claims not to remember. Locke provides no clues for establishing the verity of a person's memory claims. This is a problem that was raised by Locke's friend William Molyneux, who appealed to Locke's own example of the drunken criminal. In this example, which Locke provides in the *Essay*, chapter XXVII, section 22, a person commits a crime while intoxicated which he later claims he has no consciousness memory of committing. According to Locke, the criminal is punished in these cases precisely because courts of law have no means of discerning whether a person actually lacks consciousness of a past event or is merely claiming so. In these cases, Locke argues, the law can prove that the same man committed the crime who is presently being charged, and since lack of consciousness of the event cannot be proven, then this is the best we can do. Ultimately, he explains, God will know the truth of the matter and will act accordingly. As Locke writes, "in the great Day, wherein the Secret of all Hearts shall be laid open, it may be reasonable to think, no one shall be made to answer what he knows nothing of" (2.27.2). The upshot of this argument is that if the court could somehow get a God's-eye view of the drunkard's conscious memories, they would not punish him for what he genuinely does not recollect doing. They would have to acknowledge, as God would, that the act was performed by a different person, although the same man. Molyneux objects that the drunkard should be punished without qualification, since the drunkard voluntarily got himself drunk and therefore stands responsible for whatever he does in that voluntarily induced state of mind.[1] As we have seen, Locke thinks the decision of the court to punish the drunkard is provisional, because it is the best we can do without a God's-eye view of the drunkard's conscious memories. However, Molyneux seems to want to suggest that the drunkard be punished *even if* we were to know his claims regarding lack of consciousness were in fact true. A voluntary act is liable, and all the possible outcomes of that are liable as well, regardless of our consciousness of having done them. This example illustrates the implications of Locke's theory—while he and Molyneux agree regarding the court's decision to punish, their reasons for so doing are very different. Locke grants their partial agreement, but argues that accepting the grounds for their agreement would pose a threat to his theory. As he sees it, no matter how good a reason that might seem for punishing the drunkard, it is not a reason Locke can appeal to. He would have to concede that the drunk is the same person as the sober man, and this he is not willing to do. For the purposes of assigning blame in this case, Locke cites practical considerations alone—in other words, we punish the drunk just because we cannot know the truth of what he claims regarding his memories. This example does not amount to a serious problem for Locke, but it does underline the commitment he clearly has to tying moral responsibility to memory, if not in this life, then in the afterlife, where our hearts are finally laid bare before an omniscient God.

(b) The problem of lost memories: Reid's gallant officer

The problem of lost memories has seemed to many of Locke's critics to have even greater implications for the theory of personal identity itself, leaving aside questions of responsibility. In his work *Essays on the Intellectual Powers of Man*, Essay III, chapter 6, Thomas Reid raised this issue with the example of the gallant officer, in an effort to illustrate the absurd implications of Locke's theory for personal identity. In this example, we are to imagine a brave officer who stole apples from an orchard when he was a boy, grew up to become an officer recognized for his bravery in capturing the enemy standard, and eventually becomes a famous general in his later years. While the officer can remember being flogged as a boy, the older general no longer remembers this incident, although he does remember capturing the standard as an officer. Here we have a situation in which personal identity relations fall apart over the continuous life of the man. On Locke's account, the general is the same person as the officer, but he is not the same person as the young boy. This seemed to Reid to show that Locke's position flies in the face of any rational person's intuition regarding personal identity. Identity is transitive, Reid argues: if a is the same as b and b is the same as c, then a is the same as c. While Reid's example might succeed in proving that the theory of personal identity Locke proffers is counterintuitive, it does so only if we are presuming a commonplace conception of personal identity as pointing to a continuous physical being over time. Locke's theory of personal identity, however, does not intend to capture this kind of identity. He is explicit in establishing that *personal* identity is distinct from human identity, and while the latter establishes the continuity of a physical life, the former is meant to capture our sense of individual moral responsibility. And moral identity is not transitive, Locke thinks, in the same way as human identity is. The general, in terms of moral responsibility, remains liable and answerable for the actions of the gallant officer, but is not answerable for the actions of the young boy. They are the same man, from boyhood to old age, but the old man does not carry the weight of responsibility for what the young boy did. Reid's example does not capture this important distinction because it brackets the moral issues in an effort to get at the seeming absurdities arising from lost memories.

(c) Circularity in Locke's account: Butler's objection

Joseph Butler also sought to point out the absurdity of Locke's position, arguing that Locke's theory ends up with a vicious circularity. Butler argued that consciousness presupposes personal identity, since my having a consciousness of doing something includes the assumption that it was *I* who did it. Lurking behind the string of memories that Locke identifies as the self, there must, Butler argued, be a continuous substance that had and currently has conscious experiences. Without this metaphysical glue, so to speak, which bonds the series of past experiences together in some way that makes them mine, "our present self is not, in reality, the same with the self of yesterday, but another like self or person coming into its room, and mistaken for it; to which another self will succeed tomorrow."[2] Butler's charge against Locke is founded mainly in his conviction that the commonsense presumption each person has of being a continuous person with a substantial, continuous identity holds a great deal of validity. He argues that a person's assurance of having performed an action stands as proof that we own only the actions that we take to be ours in some substantial sense. If John owns an action he knows he performed last week, then "this he, person, or self, must either be a substance or the property of some substance."[3] If consciousness of self is taken to be a property of substance, Butler argues, then consciousness over time effectively proves substantial unity over time. For Butler, John's consciousness that he is the same property as last week is, for John, "as certain a proof that his substance remains the same, as consciousness that he remains the same substance would be."[4]

Butler is correct in stating that we all have a belief in our own continuous identity; however, his repeated assertion that these beliefs are certainties signals a fundamental misunderstanding of Locke's concerns. Butler is presuming the very thing that Locke is placing into question—the certainty with which we can assert the reality of a continuous substance that is the self. Locke's position regarding substance is that human epistemological limitations require a position of agnosticism regarding the nature and existence of substances of any kind. For Locke, the thing which underlies perceivable qualities is not something the mind can perceive, even in the case of the thinking substance itself. As Locke himself admits, he is proposing a theory that "will look strange to some Readers and possibly they are so in themselves" (2.22.27). In other words, this theory runs counter to many of our common suppositions about our own natures, and it may well be incorrect as regards the unity of the self. However, as Locke explains, it is the most plausible and defensible theory possible in light of the ignorance we are in regarding the nature of the immaterial substances. As with many aspects of Locke's *Essay*, we must bear in mind that Locke's theory of personal identity is intended not to illuminate us with regard to absolute truths regarding the world, but rather to expose unwarranted presumptions and to establish the foundations for plausible and clear ideas about the world. To this end, we must avoid obscurities in our identity talk by clearly demarcating what ideas we can have regarding persons and the distinction between that idea and the identity of material or vegetative things. Locke sees the category of person as a distinctly moral, rather than metaphysical, category. Since it is impossible that we have any direct experiential ideas of an abiding and unified self, the question of its nature must remained unanswered. What Locke offers instead is the unifying nature of consciousness, gappy as it is, to establish current and past ownership of actions.

THE GAPS IN IDENTITY AND HUME'S THEORY

One thinker who did seem to grasp the problem that Locke was dealing with is Hume, who appears to have been uniquely prepared to accept the implications of Locke's view. Hume accepted Locke's reduction of human identity to singular conscious experiences and agreed with Locke's empiricist restriction on experiential ideas. Hume's theory of identity might be seen as picking up where Locke left off—while Locke leaves us with a theory of identity that is frankly agnostic with respect to the substantial and continuous self, Hume rejects the notion altogether. There is no substantial self, according to Hume, merely a bundle of memories that the mind collects into one continuous identity by what Hume calls a "fiction" of the imagination. In this way, Hume accounts for the belief we all have in the substantial self (the belief Butler took to be a decisive blow against Locke's reductionist view), while at the same time showing that there is no real substantial self to speak of. To attribute identity to something it must be a thing whose existence is continuous and uninterrupted. Personal identity is not like this, given the gappyness of conscious experience. Strictly speaking, then, persons have no continuous identity, but are the sum of solitary experiences bundled by the mind into one thing.

Locke was unwilling completely to reject the possibility of a substantial self, but argued that we could have no direct knowledge of it. Hume employs a similar strategy to Locke's but concludes that a substantial self is no more than a fiction we believe in. Of course, both theorists had some trouble convincing readers for whom the continuity of the self is something we take for granted. Locke agreed that the theory might look strange, but argued that this is due to the ignorance we are in regarding the substance of the self. Hume, who had finally rejected the substantial self altogether, found himself in an even stranger position; he wrote in his Appendix to his *Treatise of Human Nature*, "all my hopes vanish, when I come to explain the principles, that unite our successive perceptions in our thought or consciousness. I cannot discover any theory, which gives me satisfaction on this head."[5]

Locke's apparent lack of concern about the issue, however, is best understood in light of his characterization of personal identity as a "forensick" term. For Locke, the broader question of the substantial nature of the self is one that we simply have no epistemological resources to answer. Locke is trying to locate the basis for moral responsibility rather than trying to establish a clear account of what it means to be a person in any strong metaphysical sense. Locke is concerned with what we are capable of knowing rather than what we cannot. If the essence of our identity is not knowable to us, then it is not something we need to dwell on. However—and this is important for Locke's overall project—we can know enough about human and personal identity for the practical task of assigning moral responsibility for actions done in the past.

Despite the controversy generated by Locke's account, it was, and remains, a landmark in philosophical thinking about personal identity. Locke's memory criterion set the standard for subsequent discussions of personal identity, particularly through his separation of the identity of human from the identity of person. Many critics charged that memory could not stand as the single mark of identity of persons, and yet the theory also had many adherents, and still does to this day. Some of the most influential names in modern identity theory hold some version of the psychological continuity thesis introduced by Locke.

CHAPTER FIVE

LOCKE'S THEORY OF MORALITY

Before we embark on a discussion of Locke's moral theory, it might be useful to return to that fateful conversation between Locke and his friends which Locke recounts in his *Epistle to the Reader*. According to Locke, his inspiration for exploring human understanding of issues arose as a result of this discussion, which he describes as having being *"on a Subject very remote from this"* (*Epistle*, 7). James Tyrell, one of Locke's friends in attendance that evening, later recalled that the discussion concerned morality and revealed religion. Given that Locke himself wrote that the subjects they spoke of that night were "very remote" from the matters of the *Essay*, one might conclude that morality, for one, is not a greatly significant subject of discussion with respect to this work. Yet we might wonder whether it is really such a "remote" topic after all; aspects of the *Essay* would suggest that, for Locke, moral knowledge is the crowning achievement of human reason.

THE SIGNIFICANCE OF MORALITY
IN THE *ESSAY*

Locke devotes little space in the *Essay* to moral discourse. His references to moral laws, and to moral knowledge, are occasional. There is no extended discussion of Locke's moral system, and the references he does make to his moral theory seem more like a promissory note for a more full-fledged discussion than any earnest attempt to convey his positive moral position. In fact, his friend Molyneux and his apologist Catharine Trotter Cockburn each sought to convince Locke that he ought to develop the morality hinted at in the *Essay* into a book devoted to his moral views. In her work *A Defense of Mr. Locke's "Essay of Human Understanding,"* Cockburn wrote:

> I wish, Sir, you may only find it enough worth your notice, to incite you to show the world, how far it falls short of doing justice to your principles; which you may do without interrupting the great business of your life, by a work, that will be an universal benefit, and which you have given the world some right to exact of you. Who is there so capable of pursuing to a *demonstration* those reflections on the grounds of *morality*, which you have already made?[1]

Cockburn took Locke's work to be deeply concerned with morality, but lacking the full-blown moral system of which she took his work to be suggestive. Locke never did publish such a work, though his ideas on morality figured prominently in moral debate of the eighteenth century. We might ask ourselves whether the discussion that evening at Oxford was simply a catalyst for his general epistemology or whether questions of morality (and religion) have some more central role to play in Locke's *Essay*.

There seems to be little question that Locke took morality to be the most important aspect of human intellectual and practical life. As he writes, *"Morality is the proper Science, and Business of Mankind in general"* (4.12.11). It's safe to say that the amount of attention paid to morality in the *Essay* belies its primacy in Locke's epistemological landscape. Despite its sporadic appearance in the *Essay*, morality is accorded a special place in Locke's epistemology; it is one of *"the Sciences capable of Demonstration"* (4.3.18), wherein the foundations of our moral duty can be known with certainty. Considering that this is an honor it shares only with mathematics, there is no doubt that morality is a significant category of human knowledge for Locke.

We would do well to ask ourselves why it is that Locke spends so little time developing a positive moral theory in the *Essay*, given how central it seems to be for human life. One possible answer is that Locke is not as interested in working out a moral system in the *Essay* as he is in laying the epistemological foundations for the discovery of morality. A *proper* understanding of the strengths and limits of human reason frees us from wasting our intellectual energy on achieving certainty in those things of which we can have only probable knowledge. We must, as Locke writes, "know our own *Strength*" (1.1.6) and turn our attention to those areas in which we can have certainty, that is, "those [things] which concern our Conduct" (1.1.6). The *Essay* can be seen as being broadly concerned with establishing appropriate limits on knowledge claims and paving the way for moral reasoning. That said, Locke's references to morality do suggest a specific conception of the origin of moral rules, the obligation we have to obey them, and our motivation for doing so. Before examining the various references Locke makes to morality in the *Essay*, it might first be helpful to identify Locke's general moral position, which can be broadly characterized as *natural law* theory.

LOCKE'S NATURAL LAW MORALITY

Let us begin with a brief examination of natural law theory as it was understood in the medieval and early-modern periods. It has its roots in the writings of St. Thomas Aquinas, who most famously set out the fundamentals of natural law theory. For Aquinas, natural law was a part of God's eternal law, which was God's blueprint for the rational ordering of all created things. All beings are governed by these laws as a means of ensuring the natural order. Non-rational beings participate in the natural order because they are determined by this law, as is clear from their instinctive patterns of behavior. Rational beings, on the other hand, participate in the natural order by following the principles of reason, given to us by God for this very purpose. Reason, on this view, is the faculty by which humans perceive God's laws. These laws are knowable by all rational beings, and, once known, compel the reasoner to obedience. Through reason, human beings are able to determine the naturally appropriate set of goods and how they ought to be achieved; such goods include, for Aquinas, life, marriage, social harmony and the avoidance of harm, reasonableness, and knowledge. From these basic moral goods, all others can be rationally deduced.

Locke makes certain remarks in the *Essay* that are strongly suggestive of natural law theory. These remarks focus on the rational aspect of morality and the divine origin of absolute moral rules. We can fill out Locke's natural law position by looking to an earlier, unpublished work of Locke's, entitled *Essays on the Law of Nature*. This work, written in the 1660s (roughly thirty years before the publication of the *Essay*), is a collection of essays outlining Locke's natural law position and his moral epistemology. Here he defines natural law as "the decree of the divine will discernible by the light of nature and indicating what is and what is not in conformity with rational nature, and for this very reason commanding or prohibiting."[2] Locke likens moral law to physical law. Morality is the law governing human behavior just as physical laws govern the behavior of all other things in the world. Natural law is what he calls a "plan, rule, or . . . pattern" of life.[3] These laws are discoverable by reason, and they are obligatory by virtue of their divine authority. For Locke, in this early work, these laws are the touchstone for deriving all of our moral duties— much like mathematical axioms. The moral status of any particular action is determined by comparing our behavior against the laws we deduce through reason. Much of this view remains, in bits and pieces, in the *Essay*. Here, Locke argues that the key to the discovery of moral rules is individual reason. For example, in Book IV Locke explains that our natural faculties of reasoning may not be suited to understanding the real essence of bodies, but are sufficient for ensuring the condition of "our eternal estate." He writes, "it will become us, as rational Creatures, to imploy those Faculties we have about what they are most adapted to, and follow the direction of Nature, where it seems to point us out the way" (4.12.11). For Locke, reason must discover the moral law that governs human nature and it is

> by comparing them to this law . . . that men judge of the most considerable *Moral good* or *Evil* of their Actions—that is, whether as *Duties, or Sins*, they are like to procure them happiness, or misery, from the hands of the ALMIGHTY. (2.28.8)

However, Locke's moral theory is far from straightforward. In the *Essay*, Locke also develops a *hedonistic* account of morality, which makes pleasure the standard for goodness and pain the standard for evil. The obligatory force of moral rules, on this account, arises from the pleasure that is gained, and the pain that is avoided, by our obedience to them. Morality thus reduces to the weighing of hedonistic considerations in deciding how to act. Many commentators have argued that these two distinct strains of thought in Locke's work, the rationalistic and the hedonistic, amount to a fatal tension in Locke's moral theory. Locke scholar Richard I. Aaron has summed the problem up as follows:

> Two theories compete with each other in [Locke's] mind. Both are retained; yet their retention means that a consistent moral theory becomes difficult to find. The first is hedonism, which, in Locke's writings, assumes the form that the good is whatever produces pleasure . . . the second is rationalism, the view that reason alone can determine what is truly good.[4]

LOCKE'S MORAL RATIONALISM

For a natural law theorist, the process of discovering moral laws is very important. We are easily mistaken or misled by prejudice, bias, or emotion regarding morality, and the only safeguard against error is to ensure that we restrict our moral inquiries to clear ideas and the necessary relations that hold between them. It is for this reason that Locke is so adamantly opposed to innatist or authoritarian foundations for moral belief. As Locke explains, the difference between natural law morality and moral innatism is "between something imprinted on our Minds in their very original, and something that we being ignorant of, may attain to the knowledge of, by the use and due application of our rational Faculties" (1.3.13). A theme that runs throughout the *Essay* regards the appropriate use of reason and a proper appreciation of our rational limits. In the *Essays on the Law of Nature*, Locke espouses what sounds like a decidedly Aquinian view of natural law. Here he writes that "the proper function of man is acting in conformity with reason, so much so that man must of necessity perform what reason prescribes."[5] Locke's repeated reference to the kind of knowledge our minds are best suited to or fitted for would seem to fit with the traditional rationalistic account of natural law morality.

How far does Locke's theory of moral knowledge fit the rationalist picture? In order to answer this question, it might be useful to look briefly at the epistemologies that characterize rationalists and empiricists. Rationalists, generally speaking, hold a view of knowledge according to which new ideas or relations of ideas are supplied by reason alone, and, most importantly, these are the only kinds of ideas or relations of ideas that count as knowledge. The rationalist believes the human mind can achieve certainty with regard to the kinds of propositions discovered in this manner and that these propositions enhance our understanding of the world in some respect. As an example, René Descartes held geometrical concepts to be purely rational and absolutely clear to mind. For Descartes, these concepts informed all of our most basic conceptions of the world. They were fundamental to our understanding of things. The propositions built from these rationally derived ideas are known to be true intuitively, which means that the relations between the ideas being considered are perceived to be true immediately by the mind. Other propositions, such as a long mathematical proof, for example, are discovered by deduction from these intuitive principles, and are seen by the rationalist to carry an equal level of certitude. The key feature of rationalism is that the ideas which contribute to knowledge must be ideas originating in the mind—abstract ideas that the mind understands perfectly and completely. For Descartes, these ideas had to be "clear and distinct." For this reason, most rationalists reject the validity of ideas of sensation since they are incomplete or confused. Innate ideas rationalists argue that intuitively known truths cannot be learned, in the sense of being derived from sensory ideas, but rather must be known *a priori*, as essential contents of the mind. Not all rationalists need to be innate ideas theorists, however. Others argue that our intuitive knowledge is gained by a process of abstraction from experiential ideas and intuitive perceptions about the relations between these abstract ideas. Whether innatist or not, however, rationalists all agree that the knowledge gained through the perception of relations between clear and distinct abstract ideas is superior to anything we can claim regarding sensory ideas. Abstract rational ideas inform us in ways that sensory ideas cannot, because abstract ideas are products of the mind alone.

Empiricists generally reject this high epistemic standard for knowledge. Empiricists hold that all of the ideas and propositions before the mind are derived from sensory experience. For the empiricist, reason is not a source of knowledge, but only a faculty of relating experiential ideas in a variety of ways. Reason cannot produce new ideas, according to the empiricist, and though reason can create abstract ideas from experiential ideas, these abstract ideas have no special epistemic status. They are useful means of communication and classification, but do not inform us about the world. Knowledge, *if* it is possible, can be gained only by experience, for the empiricist, and there is nothing superior that reason alone can add. The empiricist may grant, with the rationalist, that experiential ideas cannot provide us with certainty, since they are incomplete. But the empiricist will conclude that certainty is something our minds are simply incapable of having. This is the position of someone like David Hume, who held that all propositions are open to skeptical doubt. The most Hume is willing to grant regarding purely rational knowledge, such as mathematics, is that while approaching certainty, this kind of knowledge tells us nothing about the world.

Locke is an empiricist like Hume with regard to ideas of substances. As we have seen, Locke considers our substance ideas to be inadequate and that no amount of observation and experiment will reveal to our minds the real constitution of material objects. For this reason, we cannot have true knowledge about substances. However, Locke parts company with the more strictly empiricist thinkers, and starts to sound much more like a rationalist, when he talks about intuitive reasoning from ideas of modes. For Locke, modes are abstract ideas created by the mind out of experiential ideas, but referring to no extra-mental reality. As such, they are ideas we know completely and they are products of the mind alone. It is here that Locke thinks true knowledge is possible. The kinds of subjects that fall into this category are the existence of God, mathematical propositions, and moral propositions. Locke holds that moral propositions constitute an informative and practical kind of knowledge. Locke's empiricism is thus mitigated by rationalism with respect to morality. Hume, for example, grounded morality in emotion, thereby maintaining a consistently empiricist position by deriving moral concepts from feelings of empathy and repulsion. Thomas Hobbes grounded morality in hedonistic self-interest, tying good and evil to natural pleasure and pain. Locke does not take this route—at least not entirely.

Locke writes,

I am bold to think, that *Morality is capable of Demonstration*, as well as Mathematicks: Since the precise real Essence of the Things moral Words stand for, may be perfectly known; and so the Congruity, or Incongruity of the Things themselves, be certainly discovered, in which consists perfect knowledge. (3.11.16)

Locke's claim here is that moral rules can be proven with the same degree of precision and certainty as a mathematical theorem. While the basic ideas used for such proofs arise from experience, the proofs themselves deal with abstract, modal, ideas that are constructed by mind alone. Thus, moral ideas are adequate ideas, completely and perfectly transparent to the mind. In this way, Locke explains, "moral Knowledge may be brought, to so great Clearness and Certainty" (3.11.17). Like mathematics, morality can be deduced from self-evident propositions, according to Locke. He offers an example, which he claims is as certain "as any Demonstration in Euclid" (4.3.18), and it is the following: *Where there is no property, there is no injustice.* The abstract idea of property, Locke explains, is a right to something. The idea of injustice is the violation of that right. Considering these ideas together, a rational person can see that, by definition, injustice cannot exist if there is no property right to be violated. For Locke, this is as clear as any mathematical proposition. Likewise for the proposition *No Government allows absolute Liberty.* Again, Locke begins with the definition of Government as an abstract modal idea created by the mind. Government is the establishment of society upon certain laws, requiring conformity, according to Locke. Absolute liberty, again a modal idea, is defined by Locke as allowing anyone to do whatever she pleases. Since Locke thinks any rational person will perceive the disagreement of the ideas of absolute liberty and Government, the proposition under consideration is clearly true. The obvious problem with this kind of analysis is that it relies upon definitions of ideas such as Government or liberty being clear and uncontroversial.

Constructivism lies at the very heart of Locke's theory, as when he writes that the ideas of modes are "*Ideas* put together at the pleasure of our Thoughts, without any real pattern they were taken from" (4.4.12). Yet Locke is not a moral relativist. For Locke, as we have seen, murder is wrong just as squares have four right angles. Any disagreements regarding what counts as murder and what does not are resolvable by the careful definition of terms, but Locke thinks everyone can discern the wrongness of murder, and that it is deserving of capital punishment (as he claims in 4.4.8). Now, Locke's presumption of the universality of agreement with capital punishment would seem to be a clear problem for his view, since there are many people who do not see the agreement between ideas of murder and of capital punishment as a response. The account of moral knowledge he provides could end up being wholly reliant on commonly held moral conceptions rather than real moral truths, as he intends them to be. As such, morality might begin to seem somewhat arbitrary.

Locke addresses this concern by appealing again to the mathematical analogy. Mathematical ideas could not conceivably be affected by idiosyncrasy. Consider the case in which a person conceives the idea of a figure with three angles of which one is a right angle. She might call this a square or a trapezium or whatever else she likes, but, Locke points out, no matter what she calls it, the character of the angles and their relative equality is clearly understood by anyone to whom it is explained. There is a real truth, Locke explains, to the ideas of equality and the angles of a triangle, because the ideas are grasped by the mind so clearly and completely. So it is for moral concepts. We can all grasp the disagreement between the ideas of ownership and taking things without the owner's consent. According to Locke, the ideas of justice, theft, sacrilege, murder, and so on are real and true because they are purely abstract ideas. Locke thinks this point will have to satisfy the constructivist concern. We cannot simply put any ideas together and say they agree or disagree. As in math, so in morality—no matter what we call them, once the abstract ideas are understood, their agreements or disagreements will be clear and plain. No one can hold that two is equal to five, and similarly no one can hold that theft is equal to justice (at least not if those terms are perfectly understood). Of course, it seems to most people that mathematical terms are significantly less controversial than moral ones. The meaning of *triangle* will strike many readers as being easier to settle upon than the meaning of *justice*, if for no other reason than that we can simply draw one by way of conveying its meaning. Locke grants that moral terms are much less easily defined. Many different simple ideas go into the making of a complex idea such as *justice*, and people frequently join ideas to moral terms that are not relevant. However, for Locke, this is merely a problem of precision in defining our terms and does not pose any impediment to the demonstrability of moral knowledge. What Locke has in mind here is a kind of dialogic process, whereby speakers could identify the moral ideas they have in their minds and compare them to the ideas of others. Locke does not worry greatly about culturally relative moral propositions, as he thinks moral ideas are, as modal ideas, a matter of rational construction and fully transparent to any rational person who takes the time to analyze their essential components carefully. Locke acknowledges that people commonly disagree about the definition of moral ideas, but insists that if people honestly laid aside their biases and prejudices and searched after moral truth in the same way they seek out truths regarding mathematics, they would discover them to be very clear and objective ideas. Once these moral rules are known, Locke explains, they "cannot but determine the Choice in anyone, that will but consider" (2.21.70).

Part of what it means to know moral law is to understand its divine origin. As such, each rational person knows that these laws are obligatory. For example, in one passage of the *Essay*, Locke explains that while people *do* need incentive provided by rewards and punishments to obey natural law, this "takes nothing from the Moral and Eternal Obligation, which these Rules evidently have" (*Essay*, 1.3.6). In *Essays on the Law of Nature*, Locke argues that we feel an obligation to natural law not merely because sanctions are attached to divine moral law, but primarily because the moral law itself compels us. That knowledge is sufficient for a rational individual, according to Locke. He explains as follows:

> all obligation binds conscience and lays a bond on the mind itself, so that not fear of punishment, but a rational apprehension of what is right, puts us under an obligation, and conscience passes judgment on morals, and, if we are guilty of a crime, declares that we deserve punishment.[6]

For Locke, it would seem, the rational apprehension of the justice of natural law places human beings under an obligation, and it is due to this rational awareness that humans understand moral transgressions as *intrinsically* wrong.

But recall that this is not the whole story for Locke's moral theory. In the *Essay*, Locke locates the origin of our ideas of moral good and evil in empirically derived ideas of pleasure and pain, giving his theory a decidedly hedonistic quality. In the *Essay*, it becomes clear that Locke thinks reason alone, and the moral laws it discovers, cannot motivate us; we need to feel some uneasiness in the desire of some good in order to act.

LOCKE'S HEDONISM: REWARD AND PUNISHMENT

Locke does not specify any special moral faculty by which we acquire our moral knowledge. The fundamental notions of virtue and vice are founded on empirically derived ideas. In Book II of the *Essay*, Locke discusses pleasure and pain. These are simple ideas of experience, for Locke, that cannot be defined except by reflecting on how we feel at any given moment. *Good* is whatever creates pleasure in us, or a diminishment of pain. *Evil* is that which produces pain or diminishes pleasure. These are, for Locke, "very considerable" (2.20.1) ideas, as they "are the hinges on which our passions turn" (2.20.3). Pleasure and pain are equated with feelings of delight or uneasiness aroused by certain sensations or reflections. In frightening situations, for example, feelings of uneasiness are attendant on the experience in anticipation of some future pain. In joyful situations, feelings of delight are aroused by the anticipation of some future good.

Moral good and evil do not seem to be qualitatively different from pleasure and pain, on Locke's account. Goods and evils are morally significant when they involve pleasures and pains brought about by conformity or lack thereof to moral laws. Recall that, for Locke, the mind discovers moral laws and these are intended as guides to human action. Locke explains moral relations as the relations between people's voluntary actions and the rule to which they are referred. So, the abstract moral rules are the means by which we evaluate the rightness or wrongness of our actions with reference to God's will. In Book IV, Locke offers the example of what he takes to be a universal moral rule—*murder deserves death*. Once we know this proposition to be true, he explains, "it will also be true in Reality of any Action that exists conformable to that *Idea of Murther* [*sic*]" (4.4.8). Morally good or evil actions would therefore seem to be actions that either conform or do not conform to these rationally derived laws; case closed. However, for Locke, moral good and evil are basically equivalent to pleasure and pain. So, how does the moral law figure in the discernment of moral good or evil when natural good and evil seem to be our guides to action? For Locke, an action is *morally* good or evil insofar as it conforms, or fails to conform, to a law *carrying specific rewards or punishments*. As Locke explains it,

> *Morally Good and Evil* then, is only the Conformity or Disagreement of our voluntary Actions to some Law, whereby Good and Evil is drawn on us, from the Will and Power of the Law-maker; which Good and Evil, Pleasure or Pain, attending

our observance, or breach of the Law, by the Decree of the Law-maker, is that we call *Reward* and *Punishment*. (2.28.5)

Locke's moral theory is aptly termed *legalistic*, because of his general view of morality as involving sanction-backed laws from a superior with law-making authority. God, he explains, has the right to set the laws he sees fit; he "has Goodness and Wisdom to direct our Actions to that which is best: and he has Power to enforce it by Rewards and Punishments, of infinite weight and duration, in another Life" (2.28.8). The laws, therefore, which are the expression of divine will, seem to gain their obligatory *force* not solely from their divine origin, but from the fact that they are *sanction-backed* rules of a superior authority. These laws seem to carry no inherent obligatory *force* apart from the fact that they carry sanctions. It would be "utterly in vain," Locke argues, to suppose a rule to guide human actions that was not enforced by reward and punishment. For Locke, humans are motivated by fear of pain and a desire for pleasure, and he believes it to be very difficult, if not impossible, to motivate people to act on any other grounds. It would seem, then, that the laws themselves carry no motivational significance to us, except insofar as they affect our hedonistic concerns. This has seemed to many readers to lend a certain arbitrariness to the content of the laws, since their inherent righteousness does not seem to concern us in our moral decision-making. Below we will return to the consideration of Locke's more rationalistic moral theory, as there may well be a means of reconciling the inherent righteousness of moral law with Locke's legalistic hedonism. Let us turn now to Locke's theory of the will and human motivation in order to clarify Locke's hedonism.

MOTIVATION AND THE WILL

The will, for Locke, is "nothing but a power in the Mind to direct the operative Faculties of Man to motion or rest" (2.21.29). The will directs not only physical action, but also all actions of the mind—thinking of one thought or another, speaking or not speaking, believing or not believing, and so on. If we had no perception of delight, for example, Locke writes,

we should have no reason to preferr [*sic*] one Thought or Action, to another; Negligence, to Attention; or Motion, to Rest. And so we should neither stir our Bodies nor employ our Minds; but let our thoughts (if I may so call it) run a drift, without any direction or design; and suffer the *Ideas* of our Minds, like unregarded shadows, to make their appearances there, as it happen'd, without attending to them. (2.7.3)

But what motivates the mind to will one action or another? As we saw above, the key motivating factor for humans is desire for pleasure and an abhorrence of pain. However, Locke's theory is somewhat subtle on this point. We do not simply act in the pursuit of pleasure or happiness, on Locke's account. The will is motivated, for Locke, by what he terms *uneasiness*, which is a present and immediate pain in the body or an immediate disquiet of the mind. For Locke, the will is moved not by consideration of future goods, but only by immediate desires. Present feelings are the immediate causes of actions, for Locke—not rational considerations and beliefs, but present uneasiness. Consideration even of some greatest good is not going to motivate the will unless there is some felt uneasiness or desire for that good, and it is always going to be the most pressing or immediate desire that moves us to act. Locke proposes this account as a means of explaining why it is that human beings show themselves to be so ineffective in directing their wills to future goods. The threat of eternal damnation was, for Locke, a perfect example. Though a person may acknowledge the wages of sin in terms of eternal damnation, many people do not alter their behavior to ensure ultimately good outcomes and the pleasure of heavenly rewards. The problem, to Locke's mind, is not that people have not properly considered the wages of sin. Rather, Locke argues, it is that heavenly rewards do not constitute most people's immediate desires. The absence of heavenly rewards at this moment does not cause a present uneasiness. Present and immediate desires are what determine my will, and my desires center not on absent goods but on present uneasiness. The good has to be something that will alleviate present pain in order for it to have any motivational force, since, as Locke explains, "'Tis *uneasiness* determines the will . . . Because that alone is present, and 'tis against the nature of things, that what is absent should operate, where it is not" (2.21.37). The ultimate happiness to be had in heaven may, clearly to all who contemplate it, far outweigh any of the pleasures to be had here on earth, but the alleviation of immediate pains will always prevail over the will. As Locke explains,

> in full view of this difference, satisfied of the possibility of a perfect, secure and lasting happiness, and under a clear conviction, that it is not to be had here, whilst they bound their happiness within some little enjoyment, or aim of this life, and exclude the joys of Heaven from making any necessary part of it, their desires are not moved by this greater apparent good, nor their *wills* determin'd to any action, or endeavour for its attainment. (2.21.44)

To illustrate with a more mundane example, quitting smoking is a known good for one's health, but there are many people who do not feel the immediate desire to quit. The present pain in the desire to smoke is a stronger motivating factor than the desire for the future health that will be achieved by quitting. The absence of future health does not cause present uneasiness—the smoker's will is motivated by the strongest present uneasiness. Given this, it is difficult to see how people could do the morally right thing unless that action was consistent with present desires. Why, then, might I choose to donate money to charity when my strongest present desire is to buy a large-screen television? It might seem, on such an account, that people are never able to rise above their strongest present desires. But people *do* quit smoking and donate money to charity—and Locke has an account of why this is.

SUSPENSION OF THE WILL

Locke believes we are capable of resisting the force of immediate desires and of stopping them from determining our wills. Locke introduces the notion of *suspension* as a way of explaining how people can resist acting on their present strongest desires in the pursuit of some greater good. We do this by assessing the value of a given good, such as physical health, and raising in ourselves an appropriate desire for it—a desire that, in this case, will supersede the desire to smoke. As Locke writes, we can suspend action in order to contemplate "whether it be really of a nature in it self and consequences to make [us] happy, or no" (2.21.56). This good is whatever each person determines is best for her to do. We can do this by suspending *immediate* action on our strongest present desires and deferring action in order to rationally weigh all our options for good outcomes, short term and long term. As Locke writes, we "examine [our options] on all sides, and weigh them with others" (2.21.47). This does not change the fact that we are always motivated by our immediate desires, but through careful deliberation about relative goods, we can raise a present uneasiness in ourselves for distant goods that will outweigh present uneasiness for more immediate goods. We can, Locke explains, "suite the relish of our Minds to the true intrinsick good or ill, that is in things" (2.21.53). Unless this happens, distant goods are objects merely of contemplation, and are, as such, unable to raise desires in us.

It would seem that moral laws are merely "something to think about" unless there are strong motivating considerations behind them. A person makes a specifically *moral* decision when she considers her past or future actions in light of known moral rules; for example, to donate money to charity is a moral good because it is consistent with moral laws regarding aiding those less fortunate than ourselves. But, while this law reveals to us our duty to God's law (in this case, helping those in need), the bare perception of our obligation in this case can have no motivational force unless helping the needy raises immediate desires in us that equal other immediate desires (such as going out to an expensive restaurant for dinner). The natural good to be gained by forgoing the fancy dinner is not immediately as desirable. The moral good here is acting in the benefit of humanity, but what of my immediate feelings of uneasiness about that filet mignon dinner. Social injustice does not often raise the kind of uneasiness in those who are not immediately affected by it that the absence of other more immediate goods does. Either the agent would have to feel that doing her duty to others has an intrinsic pleasure *or* the rewards and punishment must have an immediate significance to the agent's hedonistic interests. Locke thinks the greatest interests of humanity *can* dovetail with a person's immediate interests, but for this to happen she must have a clear perception of the inherent benefit of performing her duties in the interests of others so that she will be uneasy in the want of social justice. It is not clear that Locke puts much faith in the agent's ability to do this without external inducements in the manner of sanctions established by the lawmaker that manipulate her present interests in socially or morally desirable ways. Locke's insistence on sanctions as a key feature of moral motivation suggests that it is very difficult, if not impossible, for people to perceive the immediate benefits to the self in acting on moral obligations alone. At this point, it looks as though Locke's moral theory involves selfish interests and their careful manipulation by a powerful God. Although Locke makes a great deal of the righteousness and truth of natural law, for all intents and purposes the laws themselves might as well be arbitrary dictates rather than inherently good rules to follow. As Locke writes, "The true ground of Morality . . . can only be the Will and Law of a God, who sees Men in the dark, has in his Hand Rewards and Punishments, and Power enough to call to account the Proudest Offender" (1.3.6).

THE RIGHTEOUSNESS OF MORAL LAW

But what of Locke's rationalistic natural law theory? How can this be made to cohere with Locke's legalistic account of natural law. While the latter suggests that morality amounts to obedience to the sanction-based laws of a superior, as we have seen, the former suggests that morality, rationally discovered, reveals our inherent obligation to divine law. If we consider what Locke has to say in the earlier *Essays on the Law of Nature*, natural law is far from arbitrary. Locke believed that natural law was reflective of human nature in the sense that the laws intended to govern us are laws specifically tailored to the disposition and temperament of human beings. He claims, for instance, that "we can infer the principle and a definite rule of our duty from man's own constitution and the faculties with which he is equipped."[7] In other words, by examining our natures, we can reason to the laws that most naturally ought to govern us. As we have also seen, there is evidence for this in the *Essay*. Here, Locke explains that our moral rules are founded in the ideas of God as a supreme being and ourselves "as understanding, rational Beings, being such as are clear in us" (4.3.18). It is the knowledge that these are God's laws, determined by God according to the specific characteristics of human nature, that lends the obligatory weight, if not motivational force, to natural law. The specific content of natural law is based on the facts of human nature, and our duty to obey natural law lies in the authority of God's will, since it is God who originally articulated the laws suitable to creatures like us. Locke repeatedly speaks of the fittingness of morality to our rational natures, as a science discoverable by reason. God fit us with rational abilities to discern our duty, and we can perceive our obligation to obey these laws on more than strictly hedonistic grounds. The fittingness and righteousness of moral law is something, it would seem, quite apart from the legalistic features of natural law involved in its proper enforcement. In fact, for Locke, our obligation to divine law is as clear to reason as a mathematical truth. The rational person will be as certain that "the inferior, finite and dependent is under an obligation to obey the supreme and infinite as he is certain to find that three, four, and seven are less than fifteen if he chooses to compute those numbers" (4.13.3). This does not involve a perception of sanctions but a consideration of our nature and that of God, and the obligations that attend the relationship between such beings. While he may require a present uneasiness to motivate him to act, the rational agent's perception of the inherent righteousness of moral law requires no such inducement.

One way of reconciling these two strains of Locke's thought is to see Locke's rationalism and his hedonism as speaking to separate aspects of morality. Locke's rationalism concerns the discovery of moral rules, and their origin in divine will. As suggested above, there seems to be a recognition of our obligations to these laws that is not strictly hedonistic. Though Locke thinks many people are incapable of recognizing the inherent righteousness of morality, this is because they have "*no* such internal Veneration for these Rules, nor so *full a Perswasion of their Certainty* and Obligation" (1.3.7). But our lack of veneration for moral rules does not affect the fact of their inherent moral authority as rules for virtuous living. We can, in principle, discern their inherent authority if we are sufficiently insightful as to their content and source; further, we can perceive the rationality of these laws as guides to action. As Locke writes in the *Essays on the Law of Nature*, "it is reasonable that we should do what shall please him who is omniscient and most wise."[8]

Locke's hedonism concerns morality as a system of law. Insofar as natural law is intended as a kind of social control, its obligatory force arises from the authority of a superior and the sanctions the laws carry. Hedonistic considerations, then, motivate moral action insofar as morality is a system of law. However, the origin of morality in human and divine nature does speak to something more than a strictly legalistic view of morality. It was important for Locke that the laws we are being motivated to obey are, themselves, righteous laws that are set down by a benevolent superior in accord with our rational natures. If these laws were the products of an evil dictator, Locke would have nothing to say about their inherent obligatoriness, nor of our internal veneration for them. Locke scholar J.B. Schneewind has characterized Locke's natural law as the arbitrary dictates of God: "The possession of unlimited power merely enables God to be at best a benevolent despot, at worst a tyrant."[9] But this seems to ignore the fact that, for Locke, the sanctions-based obedience to these laws is only one part of the story about morality that we are given in Locke's writings. In regards to moral law as the expression of God's righteousness and our duty to God on those grounds, sanctions have no intrinsic part to play. Reason, it would seem, dictates that we should follow these laws. But the question remains whether these laws can possibly have any intrinsic motivational force. It might be possible to see how Locke thinks the rational perception of her moral duties can motivate a person's will if we return to Locke's account of suspension. The rational person will, ideally, be able to perceive that obedience to divine law is in her present interest, insofar as it is an expression of her nature. In this way, she can raise in herself an uneasiness for the satisfaction of acting in a way most fitted to her own nature and that of God; as such, then, it can become a present good. Reading Locke in this way makes sense of Locke's view that rational moral rules, clearly perceived as expressions of our nature and God's righteousness, can guide human behavior: "it is appropriate for us as rational creatures to employ our faculties on what they are best adapted to, and follow the direction of nature where it seems to show us the way" (4.12.11).

CHAPTER SIX

LOCKE'S THEORY OF KNOWLEDGE

It might seem that the first three books of the *Essay* are all about knowledge. Locke argues against the validity of innate ideas in Book I, surveys the contents of the human mind in Book II, and provides an account of the language we use to express this mental content to others in Book III. Yet, for Locke, none of these discussions is about knowledge *per se.* Though these topics are all related to knowledge, they are more correctly understood as stage-setting for the investigation of knowledge itself in Book IV. Locke's intent throughout the *Essay* is to establish the boundaries of human knowledge, thereby clarifying those things of which we can be certain and those we cannot. As he explains, his goal is to explore both knowledge *and* ignorance in order that we may

> confine our Thoughts within the contemplation of those Things, that are within the reach of our Understandings, and launch not into that Abyss of Darkness (where we have not Eyes to see, nor Faculties to perceive any thing) out of a Presumption, that nothing is beyond our Comprehension. (4.3.22)

The cautionary tone of this passage is a distinctive feature of Locke's epistemology, which is committed to the general project of mapping out the proper boundaries of knowledge. What Locke offers in Book IV is a highly restrictive account of knowledge, according to which much of what we commonly judge to be true turns out not be knowledge at all. In fact, knowledge will turn out to require a great degree of insight and certitude, achievable under a specific set of epistemological conditions. The lesson of Book IV is the lesson of the *Essay* itself: to pursue what we can know and to tread carefully in our judgments regarding things we cannot. Locke is convinced that a sober assessment of the powers of the human intellect will produce more accountable science, more constructive debate, and greater intellectual responsibility.

LOCKE'S DEFINITION OF KNOWLEDGE

Locke begins Book IV by defining knowledge as

> nothing but *the perception of the connexion and agreement, or disagreement, and repugnancy of any of our Ideas.* Where this Perception is, there is Knowledge, and where it is not there, though we may fancy, guess, or believe, yet we always come short of Knowledge. (4.1.2)

Locke's stipulation that knowledge is "nothing but" the particular perception of connections between ideas indicates Locke's very restrictive conception of knowledge; in fact, it is much more stringent a conception of knowledge than most people would commonly accept. Much of what people commonly claim to have knowledge about—for example, that dogs are carnivorous—will be categorized as probability by Locke's standards (even in the case of someone who has studied dogs and has a great deal of information about them). Locke strictly distinguishes knowledge from belief on the basis of the very specific condition that knowledge requires the perception that something is or is not the case, while the latter relies on judgment. This condition has everything to do with the clarity of the ideas we possess.

The language of perception is significant within Locke's account. He makes reference to knowledge as a kind of certainty achieved "at the first sight of the *Ideas* together" (4.2.2), the mind perceiving truth "as the Eye doth light" (4.2.2). The mind is drawn toward truth, Locke explains, and recognizes it immediately. Knowledge is clear, certain, and "irresistible," forcing itself "immediately to be perceived" (4.2.2). Though it may sound like a simple analogy, his use of the term *perception* is indicative of Locke's highly individualistic conception of knowledge. For Locke, it is only the individual experience of perceiving the relation of ideas that counts as knowledge; to know something to be true, an individual must see the agreement of ideas for herself. Accepting the truth of a proposition on authority, even on very good authority, is not knowledge, for Locke. As he explains in Book I, a person may be told something, and may well believe it to be true—for example, that the three angles of a triangle are equal to two right ones—but without ever examining the proposition himself and seeing how it is that this conclusion regarding triangles has been reached, he "hath no knowledge of the truth of it; which yet his Faculties, if carefully employ'd, were able to make clear and evident to him" (1.4.22). In other words, though this person is capable of having knowledge about the features of triangles, his mere acceptance of another person's claim does not give him true knowledge about triangles. For knowledge, the individual must perceive the relations between these ideas herself. One can detect a prescriptive tone in Locke's account of knowledge. The fact that we each have the ability to discover the true relations of ideas means, for Locke, that we are not merely settling for too little; when we choose not to use reason correctly, we do a disservice to our natural abilities; as Locke explains, knowledge depends on "*the right use of those Powers Nature hath bestowed upon us*" (1.4.22). There are, it seems, two elements at play in Locke's account. For one, knowledge is desirable because truth is something rational people should value for its own sake. Further, seeking after knowledge involves a kind of rational duty. The person who believes without good reason "neither seeks Truth as he ought, nor pays the Obedience due to his Maker, who would have him use those discerning Faculties he has given him, to keep him out of Mistake and Errour" (4.17.24). So, just as perception is a private experience (e.g., I cannot have the idea of red on the basis of someone else's experience), I cannot perceive the relations between ideas on the basis of someone else's perception of them; for me to have knowledge requires that I have the perception myself. The language of perception, then, is the language of personal experience.[1]

Locke identifies two faculties of the mind by which truth and falsehood can be discerned; these are knowledge and judgment. Knowledge is the faculty whereby the mind experiences an immediacy of perception, such that it is left with no room for doubt, hesitation, or consideration of any kind. In the case of knowledge, Locke writes, the mind "is undoubtedly satisfied of the Agreement or Disagreement of any *Ideas*" (4.14.4). Judgment, on the other hand, is the faculty whereby the mind can draw presumptive comparisons between its ideas. In cases of judgment, the certain agreement or disagreement of ideas is "not perceived, but presumed to be so" (4.14.4). For Locke, knowledge provides certainty and judgment probability. This mutually exclusive distinction of knowledge and judgment might strike the reader as odd, since we generally take knowledge to involve a kind of judgment regarding truth or falsity. The distinction Locke makes suggests that knowledge does not involve judgment, nor does it seem to involve belief. But, we might ask, what could it mean to say that one knows something without judging or believing it to be true? One way of making sense of Locke's distinction is to think about knowledge and belief in terms of grounds for assent or affirmation. Locke is trying to point to a fundamental difference in the grounds we have for taking something to be true. In the case of knowledge, the agreement of ideas is obvious to the mind solely on the basis of the ideas themselves. The perception that three is equal to three, for example, is immediate because the ideas themselves are clear and distinct before the mind; it is analytical, in other words, since it is true by virtue of the meaning of the concepts alone. My perception of the truth of the proposition is immediate, and my assent to its truth is necessary. In the case of judgment, on the other hand, I assent to the agreement of ideas on the basis of something extraneous to the ideas themselves that induces us to believe them to agree. For example, if I am considering the ideas *dog* and *carnivore*, I cannot perceive an immediate agreement of these ideas on the basis of a straightforward comparison of the ideas themselves. I need to appeal to observation, experience, or the testimony of other people. This truth of this agreement is, in some sense, synthetic, since the meaning of the ideas themselves does not reveal their agreement; my assent is based on appeals to something other than the ideas themselves, and is neither as immediate nor necessary as in the case of knowledge (I could change my mind in light of new evidence, for example). Thus, in the case of judgment, I lack what Locke calls "intuitive Evidence" (4.16.5), which is the self-contained analytical perception accorded only to knowledge.

THE DEGREES OF KNOWLEDGE

For Locke, knowledge varies in the degrees of immediacy with which relations of ideas are perceived to agree or disagree. Locke identifies three kinds of knowledge: intuitive, deductive, and sensitive. The highest degree of certainty is found in *intuitive* knowledge, where there is a direct and obvious relation between the ideas being considered. That white is not black is a disagreement directly perceived by the mind to be true. The identity of each these ideas and their distinction from one another are evident and obvious to anyone who considers them in relation to one another. This kind of knowledge, as Locke puts it, "forces it self immediately to be perceived, as soon as ever the Mind turns its view that way" (4.2.1). The greatest certainty we have is based on the intuitive perception that two ideas compared are the same or different. Of course, this level of certainty is achieved only when the ideas under consideration are absolutely clear and the distinctions between them unambiguous. This is going to be an important feature of Locke's conclusions regarding knowledge, and we will return to this below.

The perception of agreement or disagreement is not always immediate, however, as is the case with demonstrative knowledge. Here, we can perceive agreement or disagreement clearly, but not right away. For example, the perception that the sum of the three angles of a triangle is equal to the idea of the sum of two right angles is not immediate. However, if we apply intervening ideas, all themselves analytically true, by way of a proof, or *demonstration*, as Locke terms it, then we can see plainly that these ideas agree. Though it is less direct than intuitive knowledge, we end up with virtually the same degree of certainty once we have worked carefully, "by steps and degrees" (4.2.4) to the final conclusion of the proof. Locke is hesitant to impute the same degree of certainty to demonstrative knowledge, since proofs can be complex and long and require a good memory. Once the conclusion has been reached, we have to trust to the soundness of our perceptions at each step. That said, the proof is built from a series of analytically true propositions. As long as we are very attentive to all the aspects of a proof, then we can claim to have certainty regarding the agreement or disagreement of the ideas under consideration. Demonstration and intuition are the two kinds of knowledge we have, Locke asserts, and "whatever comes short of one of these, with what assurance soever embraced, is but Faith, or Opinion, but not Knowledge" (4.2.14).

There is a third kind of knowledge, which Locke identifies as sensitive knowledge. This kind of knowledge is different from intuition and demonstration as it concerns the knowledge of existence rather than the more strict agreement or disagreement of ideas. As Locke defines it, sensitive knowledge concerns "the existence of particular external Objects, by that perception and Consciousness we have of the actual entrance of *Ideas* from them" (4.2.14). What Locke is attempting to capture here is the degree of certainty we have regarding the existence of particular things. It is important to note that Locke is not talking here about ideas themselves as providing knowledge of existence. For example, I can sit in my office and call up the idea of a sandy beach I went to last summer, but the idea itself does not carry with it any guarantee that the beach actually exists. Granted, there is a high degree of likelihood that it does; in fact, I work on the assumption it does when I book my summer vacation. But the idea itself does not provide me with the certainty of a thing's existence; there is no necessary connection, as Locke puts it, between the idea of the beach and its existence at this moment. If this is the case, how does Locke think we can have knowledge of existence from the ideas of sensation? Such knowledge arises at the moment of perception, when the thing makes itself perceived by us. Thus, the idea of existence is found not in the idea itself, but in the act of *receiving* the idea. Sensory ideas are involuntary; they intrude on the mind, if you will. For example, I have ideas of my computer, the sound of the keys, and the hum of the hard drive, all of which I know to be emanating from something external to my mind; in fact it is very difficult for me to imagine that these ideas have no external cause. The evidence, Locke thinks, places this beyond doubt. Consider the difference between actually smelling a rose and remembering smelling a rose. When an idea comes into my mind through the sense, it is a palpably distinct experience from my memory or imagination of such an idea. The obtrusiveness of the experience itself makes us certain of the existence of things external to the mind. Sensation does not tell us anything about the cause of the idea, or how the external object creates the ideas in us, but it does assure us that something exists. The obtrusiveness of sensation is what makes it a kind of knowledge for Locke.

Since we have sensitive knowledge only at the moment when the idea enters the mind, sensitive knowledge only "*extends as far as the present Testimony of our sense*, employ'd about particular Objects, that do then affect them, *and no farther*" (4.11.9). If I see a person, for example, I am at the moment of perception certain that she exists right now. However, in five minutes' time, when I no longer see her, I cannot be certain that she still exists; there is no necessary connection between her existence five minutes ago and the present moment. Limited as sensitive knowledge is, it is of considerable importance, for Locke, in establishing the epistemological grounds for holding that sensation is caused by extra-mental things. Locke has in mind here the skeptical doubts posed by Descartes in his *Meditations*. Descartes famously posed a challenge to sensitive knowledge, arguing that we have no way of distinguishing dream experiences from real ones; in fact, we cannot know that our sensory ideas have not originated in the mind itself without any external cause. Anyone who makes this argument, Locke writes, "may please to dream that I make him this Answer" (4.2.14). Locke promptly dismisses Descartes' objection, on the grounds that there is no problem, for the vast majority of people at least, in making the distinction between dreams and reality. There is, he writes, a "very manifest difference between dreaming of being in [a] Fire, and being actually in it" (4.2.14). The perception of pain in the case of a real fire leaves us with no reason to doubt that it is an idea caused in us by some external object. Our ground for this certainty is our consciousness of the *entrance* of the idea into the mind as the effect of some external cause. Though it might be possible to concoct scenarios that raise doubts about the existence of things, Locke thinks there is good reason to rely upon the testimony of sensation. Apart from the absurdity of asserting that our sensory ideas are "nothing more but *Ideas* floating in our Minds" (4.11.6), Locke maintains that it is simply too difficult to doubt that our sensory ideas inform us of the existence of the things we see and feel. For Locke, a key feature of knowledge is the undeniability of the truth once it is perceived. Withholding assent in the first two cases amounts to a contradiction, and in the case of sensitive knowledge to an absurdity. Though he thinks there is assurance enough in having the experiences themselves that most people would not doubt of the truth of existence, Locke offers four reasons to trust the senses in this regard, which he thinks might aid in disabusing someone of doubts.

First, he points to the fact that people without certain senses lack the related ideas. A blind person has no ideas of color, for example. The reason for this has to be that ideas of color are produced in the mind by something outside the mind. The eyes themselves do not produce the color idea, or we would be able to see colors in the dark. Second, sensory ideas are involuntary. While I can recall the

smell of the ocean or the flavor of a pineapple at my leisure, immediate ideas of sensation are forced upon the mind, as Locke puts
it, and I cannot avoid having them. When one bites into an apple,
for example, one cannot make it taste like a pineapple. We cannot dictate the terms of sensory ideas. There must, then, be some
extra-mental thing that acts on my sensory organs. Third, Locke
appeals to the example of pain, since this is the most invasive and
unpleasant sensory experience we can have. The memory of pain
and actually having the pain are very different things. Finally, the
testimony of multiple sensations serves to confirm the existence
of things. If I see a fire, and, in that moment, doubt that it really
exists, I can stick my hand into it and feel the pain of it as well.
Sensory ideas, then, cannot be merely "the Sport and Play of my
own Imagination" (4.11.7).

Despite the fact that Locke offers up these four justificatory reasons for the existence of extra-mental object, he seems, first and
foremost, to consider sensitive knowledge to be something immediate. It relies upon no judgments or deliberations (except for the
perverse doubts of a certain few people). Sensations *are* primitive,
for Locke; my immediate experience of red, for example, carries
intrinsic evidence for the particular existence of some physical
body. However, we might still ask how this counts as knowledge,
for Locke, in anything like the way that intuition or demonstration
does? Sensitive knowledge does not seem to involve an agreement
or disagreement of ideas in the way that intuitive and demonstrative knowledge do, and Locke never attempts to explain sensitive
knowledge in these terms. It is not analytical knowledge in the same
way as these other kinds of knowledge, and our failure to assent
to the truth of existence does not amount to a contradiction in
the same way as the failing to assent to intuitive or demonstrative
truths does. Locke brackets sensitive knowledge as the least certain kind of knowledge, since it concerns existence of particular
things as opposed to general ideas. That said, Locke does suggest
that sensory experiences, as events that "obtrude" (2.1.25) on the
mind, carry with them the idea of an external cause. Sensory perception, in some sense, contains the idea of existence. The analytic-
ity of sensitive knowledge is not well developed in Locke's text, and
it might be that he is considering existence to be something other
than strictly analytic. Be that as it may, Locke concludes that the
idea of existence as it arises from sensation "is an assurance that

deserves the name of Knowledge" (4.11.3). It carries sufficiently great likelihood that puts us past doubt.

Locke's account of sensitive knowledge must be understood as a fairly restricted and bare knowledge of existence. The cause of these ideas is not known, and our complex ideas constructed from the simple ideas of experience are inadequate to constitute certainty with regard to the real unities of properties that exist outside the mind. Thus, considering his caution with regards to our knowledge of real essences, we have to be careful not to read too much into what Locke says here on the subject of sensitive knowledge. Locke is careful not to say anything here about the representational accuracy of our sensitive ideas beyond their reports of the existence of extra-mental objects. He is merely asserting that the perceptual experiences themselves strongly suggest the existence of some extra-mental cause—strongly enough, in fact, that we can call this a species of knowledge.

REALITY OF KNOWLEDGE

Locke's definition of knowledge as the perception of agreement or disagreement of ideas suggests that knowledge is something subjective, involving nothing more than drawing comparisons within the limited sphere of our own ideas. What purpose can knowledge of this sort actually serve? Locke acknowledges this concern, suggesting that it may appear he has done nothing more than build a "Castle in the Air" (4.4.1). Is Locke's theory too restricted to ideas for knowledge to be at all informative vis-à-vis the nature of objective reality? Locke addresses this concern in chapter IV, where he poses the critic's concern as follows: "[I]f there be a sober and a wise Man, what difference will there be, by your Rules, between his Knowledge, and that of the most extravagant Fancy in the World" (4.4.1)? In other words, if I compare my ideas of unicorns and serpents, or of circles and squares, what stops me from saying that I have attained knowledge in both cases on Locke's account? If knowledge is simply a matter of finding agreements or disagreements of ideas, then the claim that a unicorn is not a serpent is as certain as the claim that a square is not a circle. The fact is that if both kinds of observations have the same degree of intuitive certainty, then knowledge is potentially indistinguishable from flights of imagination. Locke must distinguish knowledge from fancy by showing that knowledge is something different, which actually does inform us about reality in a way that pure constructions of the imagination do not. He must, as Locke puts it himself, show that knowledge does not begin and terminate with our own ideas, but rather that knowledge "goes a little further than bare Imagination" (4.4.2). Given the constraints of Locke's definition of knowledge, it might seem that Locke has set himself a difficult task. He needs to provide some means of building into his definition some sense of knowledge as concerning the reality of things.

To Locke's mind, this issue does not require a reformulation of his definition of knowledge, but rather an amendment to it. Locke does this by marking out the special category of *real* knowledge, which is something more than merely the perception of agreement or disagreement of ideas (we might think of the latter as a general definition of knowledge). This special kind of knowledge requires that the ideas being compared conform to reality, and Locke thinks this kind of knowledge carries a level of certainty beyond anything that falls under his more general definition. Locke marks out the distinction of knowledge, in general, and real knowledge as follows: "Wherever we perceive the Agreement or Disagreement of any of our *Ideas* there is certain Knowledge: and where-ever we are sure those *Ideas* agree with the reality of Things, there is certain real Knowledge" (4.4.18). It is in this, he continues, that "*Certainty, real Certainty*" (4.4.18) exists.

But what will be the criterion for identifying real knowledge when we only ever directly perceive our own ideas and not things themselves? Locke identifies two kinds of ideas that he thinks can be shown to agree with the reality of things. First, there are simple ideas, which we know are produced in our minds by things outside the mind. The mind cannot produce these ideas by itself (recall Locke's example of imagining being in a fire, which is in no way the same as actually being in a fire). Our simple ideas cannot be figments of our imagination for the reason that experience itself carries the certainty of external causation in a way that imagination, he thinks, never can. Our idea of whiteness, for example, clearly indicates a power in some external body to produce that effect in us; it has a real conformity with extra-mental objects. The conformity, as Locke puts it, between sensory ideas and the existence of objects makes sensory knowledge a kind of real knowledge. However, the knowledge of material things, as we have seen, does not go any further than this. Locke excludes knowledge of complex ideas of substances as a category of real knowledge, since they are intended to represent unified entities existing outside the mind and provide us with sensitive knowledge. Since there is no way of discerning the degree to which our ideas conform with external reality, our complex ideas of substances do not constitute real knowledge. In fact, the only thing that distinguishes complex ideas of substances from ideas of imaginary beings is the stronger empirical support for the former. Legitimate, as opposed to imaginary, ideas of substance are based on unities of ideas that we have observed to come from nature, and this is where sensitive knowledge helps out. The complex idea of my cat arises from the many direct experiences I have had of its qualities, which confirm its existence as a material thing. The constant conjunction of simple ideas it always forces on my mind, coupled with my sensitive knowledge, leads me to conclude with some confidence that there is an existing thing that has those qualities. The fact that neither I nor anyone else I know of has ever had the involuntary experience of the existence of something producing unicorn ideas in our mind leads me to suspect that it is pure fancy.

But there *are* complex ideas that count as real knowledge. For Locke, there are three classes of complex idea: of modes, of relations, and of substances. Of these three, the ideas of modes and relations refer to archetypes of the mind's own making. Our ideas of modes and relations are not intended as representations of substances, so they can represent things as they really are, in their essence. At this point, we can begin to see that Locke's earlier statement that knowledge is real when it agrees with the *reality of things* is not to be taken as a literal reference to the extra-mental reality of things in the case of complex ideas. Reality, for Locke, is used here to indicate a conceptual grasp of essences. A modal idea is one that includes a clear understanding of the essential simple ideas it comprises, and the necessary connections between its simple ideas. The mind constructs these ideas freely, if you will, and as a result has a complete understanding of all the simple ideas that are required of, and necessary to, the complex idea itself. In this sense, for Locke, these ideas have reality; they fully represent their archetypes; in other words, they fully capture the essence of what they are meant to represent. In these ideas, Locke writes, "we cannot miss of a certain undoubted reality" (4.4.5). Real knowledge, in the case of intuitive and demonstrative knowledge, requires that our ideas exactly correspond to their archetypes.

What ideas are going to fall under this category? The first kind are mathematical ideas. A mathematician contemplates the properties of a rectangle or a triangle and regardless of whether there exist things outside the mind that have these properties, the knowledge that circles, as complex ideas created by the mind, have all and only the properties attributed to them is true and certain. Mathematicians need not concern themselves with the actual existence of squares or circles in the natural world, but only with the abstract definitions of the ideas of squares and circles. Their concerns focus on the ideas themselves and proofs that can be made regarding their essential features. Once these concepts are understood, the mathematician can identify things in the material world as square or round, but she does so only because she has the abstract ideas firmly in her mind. The relevant point here is that mathematical ideas are not intended to represent mind-independent things; if they do that is fine, but if they do not (as, for example, in the case of a thousand-sided chiliagon) this has no relevance to the completeness and clarity of our mathematical archetypes. These ideas answer to an archetype created by the mind and, as such, constitute real knowledge under Locke's definition.

Locke goes on to make what many have seen as a substantially more controversial claim regarding morality. For Locke, recall, moral ideas are mixed modes, and as such they are ideas created entirely by the mind out of the simple ideas of sensation. But, as mixed modes, more importantly, they are ideas that are not intended as signs of anything outside the mind. If we consider the difference between the idea of justice and the idea of a unicorn, we can appreciate the distinction Locke is trying to make here. While both ideas are created by the mind, the idea of a unicorn is the idea of a thing, and as such includes the notion of substance. Though unicorns, in most people's minds at least, fail to represent any real unity of qualities in nature, they are nevertheless ideas that are intended as a representation of substance, and, therefore, they do not fully represent their archetype (substance is an archetype created by nature and one we do not fully understand). *Justice*, conversely, is like a mathematical idea, in that it represents an archetype created wholly by the mind. Moral ideas are *"Archetypes* themselves" (4.4.7), as Locke puts it. Locke draws an analogy between moral ideas and mathematical ideas. In the same way, Locke argues, that mathematicians concern themselves with matters abstracted from the material world, so moralists concern themselves with the truth or falsity of propositions built from abstract moral ideas that do not concern the "Lives of Men, and the Existence of those Vertus in the World, whereof they treat" (4.4.8). This may sound like a very strange claim to make regarding moral rules. But Locke is making an interesting point here about moral theory—the question of the moral rightness or wrongness of abortion, for example, is not settled on the basis of there being people who actually perform or have abortions. The moral status of abortion is decided by considering abstract ideas of rights, killing, life, and the like. Likewise, we can engage in a discourse regarding the moral status of an act like cloning dinosaurs or, more fantastically, mining the resources of distant planets, even if there is no one who has actually done this. We determine our moral rules on the basis of abstract archetypes, and then we apply these to actions that exist in the mind-independent world. As Locke explains, "If it be true in Speculation, *i.e.* in *Idea*, that *Murther deserves Death*, it will also be true in Reality of any Action, that exists conformable to that *Idea* of *Murther*" (4.4.8). Because these archetypes are perfectly known, we can, with certainty, see that our ideas agree with reality (insofar as "reality" is taken in the Lockean sense), and moral knowledge therefore satisfies the requirements of real knowledge.

KNOWLEDGE OF SUBSTANCES

Locke's general definition of knowledge imposes a high epistemic standard on what will fall under the category of knowledge and what will not. Recall that, for Locke, knowledge requires that perception of the agreement or disagreement of ideas be intuitive, or at least demonstrable from intuitive propositions. Ideas of substances are going to fall short of satisfying Locke's rigorous epistemic conditions for knowledge. Substance ideas are complex ideas that aim to represent things as they exist in the natural world. Since we cannot have ideas regarding the real constitution of material objects, we lack information regarding the necessary connections between the qualities we take things to have. This is the central difference between ideas of substances and ideas of mathematics and morality. The latter ideas are so perfectly understood that the agreements or disagreements we discover involve only the general ideas themselves and not the mind-independent nature of moral acts or geometrical figures. Their archetypes are completely transparent to the mind. However, in the case of substances, our knowledge involves the comparison of ideas as they may or may not coexist in physical objects. For example, we have empirical grounds for including the ideas of solidity and four-leggedness in our complex idea of a cat, but we are not able to say with *certainty* that these qualities have a necessary unity in a single substance. We have no ideas regarding the connection between the perceivable qualities of a thing and its unperceivable qualities. We will never know, he explains, how color, taste, or sound are produced by the size and motion of particles. There is, therefore, "no conceivable *connexion* betwixt the one and the other" (4.3.13). For this reason, Locke thinks we are never going to achieve a science (in the strong sense denoting certainty) of natural bodies, concluding that it is a "lost labour to seek after it" (4.3.29). The best we can attain is an empirically based set of judgments regarding the natural world. The knowledge of things as they exist in themselves—their real constitution and properties—eludes us. That said, we must not suppose that Locke is dismissive about judgment or about the importance of scientific inquiry. The point to be taken from Locke's discussion is that our investigations of the natural world must be undertaken with a proper appreciation of the limits to our knowledge of natural things. To make Locke's position on knowledge of substances clearer, let us turn to his account of judgment.

JUDGMENT AND PROBABLE KNOWLEDGE

Locke's definition of knowledge leaves out many of the propositions we take to be true on a daily basis. As Locke himself asserts, knowledge is "very short and scanty" (4.14.1). If we were restricted to clear perceptions of the agreement or disagreement of ideas in guiding our assent we would "be often utterly in the dark, and in most Actions of [our] Life, perfectly at a stand" (4.14.1). Luckily, however, we are not limited to knowledge, but have the faculty of judgment to step in and guide assent where certainty is wanting. Judgment does not involve clear perception, since we do not immediately "see" the agreement or disagreement of ideas, but, less stringently, it involves the supposition of agreement or disagreement; it is a faculty we employ to discern probabilities, rather than absolute truths, comparing ideas and judging them to agree or disagree on the basis of likelihood, rather than intuition or demonstrative proof. Judgment is our faculty for making reasonable conjectures where certainty is wanting, and this involves the existence of things in the natural world, their constitution, properties, and the effects of their motions. While sensitive knowledge can provide certainty of the existence of things, it is much too narrow in its scope to do the job. Recall that sensitive knowledge gives us assurance of the existence of things, but only in the context of present and immediate sensations. It is for precisely this reason that Locke thinks judgment is so central. It provides us with probable knowledge, such that we can safely presume things necessary to daily life, such as being confident in the continued existence of objects that are not presently perceived, or that bread will nourish me instead of making me ill.

Locke defines probability as the appearance of agreement or disagreement of ideas that, while not perfectly clear, is sufficiently plausible to "induce the Mind to *judge* the proposition to be true, or false" (4.15.1). Probability is the likelihood of something being true—it is persuasive without being certain. The strength of our assent will depend on the level of evidence we have for the supposed agreement or disagreement of ideas. Locke identifies the degrees of assent to probable judgments as belief, conjecture, guess, doubt, wavering, distrust, and disbelief, all on a decreasing scale of evidentiary support. Probability, for Locke, fills the gaps between our sensory ideas, and guides us in cases where we have not certainty but rather a strong inducement to assent.

Locke identifies two grounds for assent to probable knowledge. The first is the conformity of a proposition to our own knowledge or experience. For example, if I live in the far north of Canada, and someone claims that there was a rain storm on a recent January afternoon, I am likely to find this improbable—not only do rain storms never happen where I live on January days, but I had no affirming experience of the rain storm myself. A second ground for assent to probable knowledge, however, involves testimony. If I am told by a great number of people that, despite the fact that the temperature was well below freezing, it did in fact rain yesterday afternoon, I am likely to find the claim more probable. If I hear a radio announcer, in an interview with a meteorologist, talking about this freakish weather incident, then I will likely impute an even greater probability to the claim, and my assent will be strengthened. The radio announcer carries, as Locke would say, a certain level of integrity and the meteorologist has a level of knowledge that lend authority to their claims about the rain storm. I have moved from distrust to doubt to belief on the basis of evidence that has strengthened the agreement of the ideas of rain and northern Canadian January weather patterns. But my assent needs to be rational, Locke warns. I must examine all the evidentiary and testimonial grounds for affirming an agreement of ideas, in order to judge confidently its relative probability. Radio announcers have been known to make mistakes, and large groups of people can believe very strange and unacceptable things. However, putting all of my sources together, including a scientist whose credentials are weighty, might induce me to assent despite the fact that the proposition itself does not in any way conform to my experience or to my minimal knowledge of patterns of precipitation in below-freezing conditions. On the other hand, propositions about alien abduction also do not, thankfully, conform to my experience or, for that matter, to that of anyone I know. While many people do believe these claims to be true, there are many people who do not think the testimony sufficiently convincing to prompt their assent. Such claims carry a lower degree of evidentiary and testimonial support, and for this reason many people remain at a level of doubt or distrust about such events.

Probability, like knowledge, involves individual reasoning. The difference in the case of probability is that we are dependent on empirical evidence and the testimony of others in determining the truth or falsity of propositions. It is, therefore, in cases of probability that people are most susceptible to dogmatic or authoritarian persuasion. It is in assessing the evidentiary grounds to which we appeal in formulating judgments, then, that assent can be regulated, or, as Locke puts it, where it "ought to be *regulated*" (4.16.1). There is a decidedly prescriptive tone to Locke's writing about knowledge and belief. Locke often speaks of assent to probabilities in terms of a rational obligation to search after truth. He speaks of loving truth for its own sake, and making proper use of the God-given faculty of reason. Locke acknowledges that it is often very difficult to ensure the grounds for one's beliefs, and it requires a great deal of intellectual work to reach a point of demonstrative certainty with regard to morality. With respect to matters of probability, Locke thinks we must do what we can in the way of scrutinizing the grounds for our beliefs, thus ensuring, to the greatest degree possible, that we avoid the pitfalls of dogmatism or the influence of authoritarianism.

FAITH

Religious belief is a special kind of belief that is grounded not in probability, but in faith. Faith is a ground for assent that does not involve rational considerations of evidence, but instead involves assenting on the basis of divinely inspired testimony alone. But Locke is careful to warn us about the dangers of taking faith as a blank check for any and all beliefs that lie outside the reach of probabilistic reasoning. Unless we are clear on precisely when faith can justifiably guide belief in the absence of rational evidence (and, for Locke, this is going to an extremely rare occurrence), we run a serious risk of believing any extravagant and absurd opinion that is concocted in the name of religion. Religions, he asserts, seem to content to appeal to reason to ground their beliefs, but are frequently resistant to holding reason as standard for reining in their assent. When they cannot make rational sense of their beliefs, they will claim that reason has no role to play in religion, claiming that matters of faith are, as Locke puts it, *"above Reason"* (4.18.2). Locke's discussion of faith is an attempt to properly mark out the realms of faith and reason.

Locke begins by setting out definitions of faith and reason. The distinction Locke draws initially might seem to suggest that faith is a matter of assenting to beliefs without rational justification. Locke defines reason as "the discovery of the Certainty or Probability of such Propositions or Truths, which the Mind arrives at by Deductions made from such *Ideas* it has got by use of its natural Faculties" (4.18.2). Faith, on the other hand, is

the Assent to any Proposition, not thus made out by the Deductions of Reason; but upon the Credit of the Proposer, as coming from GOD, in some extraordinary way of Communication. This way of discovering Truths to Men we call *Revelation*. (4.18.2)

The defining feature of faith is its reliance on testimony, and Locke's ensuing discussion concentrates on the relative legitimacy of the kinds of testimony on which faith-based belief is justified.

Locke's examination of these testimonial grounds focuses on enumerating the limits on what can count as reliable testimony and what cannot. The standard for reliable testimony, as it turns out, is going to be reason.

The testimony that faith primarily relies upon is revelation from God. What Locke sets out to do, then, is to establish when revelation is genuine and when it is not. First and foremost, Locke argues, revelation cannot inform us or enlighten us if it is cast in terms for which we have no corresponding simple ideas. Right away, Locke employs the language of reason to assess reliable testimony; the standard of reason here does not require a deductive proof, but more generally places certain requirements on the language of revelation in accordance with the ideas we have by way of our natural faculties. Any claim to revelation that involves meaningless terminology or mysterious ideas cannot reasonably form the basis for our assent. This is an important condition, since it has the further implication that any revelatory claim that is qualified to ground our assent is a claim involving ideas we already possess. For this reason, Locke argues that any proposition that can legitimately ground our faith-based assent is one that any rational person could, at least in principle, discover through reason in the absence of revelation. God might reveal the truth of a Euclidean proposition, for example, but rational individuals are capable of using their natural faculties to discover this by themselves. Locke goes so far as to say that "there is little need or use of *Revelation*, GOD having furnished us with natural, and surer means to arrive at the Knowledge of them" (4.18.4). Discovery of religious truths is, in fact, best done by reason. Locke argues that we will have more certainty of the truth of a proposition through the distinct perception of the agreement of ideas than we could ever have by basing our assent on revelatory testimony alone. Thus, the truths of revelation are clearer in our minds if they are assented to on the basis of rational demonstration or experience.

By the same principle, Locke argues, no revelatory claim can obligate our assent if it contradicts reason. As Locke writes, "*Faith* can never convince us of any Thing, that contradicts our Knowledge" (4.18.5). For example, no amount of religious authority will succeed in convincing me that two plus two equals five. Reason simply cannot accept that as true, and an appeal to faith cannot justify accepting what flies in the face of reason. Since there is great scope for doubt regarding legitimate revelation and the interpretation thereof, we have grounds for dismissing as revelatory that which is contradictory to reason. We are under no obligation, Locke asserts, to quit reason in the name of matters of faith. When we fail to apply the appropriate rational standards to revelation, we lose our ability to distinguish legitimate testimonial grounds for faith. Locke's discussion of faith is an effective attack on religious authoritarianism. His insistence on reason as the proper means of restraining assent points to individual reason as the basis for belief in matters of religion.

For someone to accept the truth of a proposition beyond its evidentiary justification signals, for Locke, an irrational motivation, arising from our passions or particular interests. One such hazard is what Locke calls enthusiasm, which is a claim to individual religious authority based on direct communications with God. While Locke does not want to deny that God has had direct communications with people, he accepts these instances only on the basis of the supporting evidence found in Scripture, and the reasonableness of these revelations. For example, the Ten Commandments were directly communicated by God to Moses. But in this case, not only is the event well documented in the Bible, but these are all rules that make sense to reason (at least as far as Locke was concerned). If the revelation is not obviously true to reason, or if it is inconsistent with experience, then we require some evidence that it is something originating from a divine source in order to be able to assent to it. But, in cases of enthusiasm, the grounds for this presumption amount to nothing more than the enthusiast's own confidence that these revelations were divine and not the product of her over-heated imaginations. The result, if direct revelation is not sufficiently scrutinized, is a fervent commitment on the part of the enthusiast, and her followers, to irrational propositions "arising from the Conceits of a warmed or over-weening Brain" (4.19.7). This state of mind is, he grants, alluring, and the ease with which an individual can convince herself that her fanciful notions are the dictates of God makes her resistant to hearing rational objections.

We can see this discussion as forming part of Locke's larger view of probability and rational responsibility. The enthusiast's problems are the same problems any of us are at risk of falling into where we fail properly to subject our beliefs to high enough evidentiary standards. Probable judgments are only as reliable as the evidence upon which they are based, and to the greatest degree possible, every rational person should endeavor to withhold assent when the evidence presented is not conclusive. A problem the enthusiast presents, however, is her own dogged assurance of the divinity of the revelation made to her. In this case, the evidence is conclusive from the perspective of the enthusiast. What Locke might say here is that we would not worry about enthusiasm if the enthusiast's claims were actually rational ones. We could accept her pronouncements regardless of their origin. If irrational, then Locke thinks we have good reason to suspect the validity of the revelation, particularly if the enthusiast can offer nothing more than her own assurance by way of evidence for her communication with God.

NOTES

INTRODUCTION

1. Thomas Hobbes. *Leviathan*, revised edition, ed. Richard Tuck. Cambridge: Cambridge University Press, 1996: 462.

CHAPTER ONE   LOCKE'S THEORY OF IDEAS

1. Edward Stillingfleet. *Origines Sacrae.* Oxford: Clarendon Press, 1797: 438.
2. Ibid.
3. Ralph Cudworth. *The True Intellectual System of the Universe*, vol. 2. New York: Gould and Newman, 1838: 136.
4. Ibid., 409.
5. John Smith. *Select Discourses.* Cambridge: Cambridge University Press, 1859: 14.
6. Nicholas Wolterstorff. *John Locke and the Ethics of Belief.* Cambridge: Cambridge University Press, 1996: 87.
7. W.K. Clifford. *The Scientific Basis of Morals.* New York: Humboldt Publishing Company, 1884: 28.

CHAPTER TWO   LOCKE'S THEORY OF MATTER

1. John Locke. "Mr. Locke's Reply to the Right Reverend the Lord Bishop of Worcester's Answer to His Second Letter," in *Some Familiar Letters between Mr. Locke, and Several of His Friends.* London: For A. and J. Churchill, 1699: 375.
2. Ibid.

CHAPTER THREE   LOCKE'S THEORY OF LANGUAGE

1. John Stuart Mill. *A System of Logic, Ratiocinative and Inductive.* London: Longmans, Green and Co., 1884: 57.

CHAPTER FOUR   LOCKE'S THEORY OF IDENTITY

1. William Molyneux. "Letter of December 23, 1693," in *Some Familiar Letters between Mr. Locke, and Several of His Friends*, London: For A. and J. Churchill, 1708: 66.

2. Joseph Butler. *Analogy of Religion.* New York: Harper & Brothers, 1860: 326.
3. Ibid., 328.
4. Ibid.
5. David Hume. *A Treatise of Human Nature*, ed. P.H. Nidditch. Oxford: Clarendon Press, 1978: 636.

CHAPTER FIVE   LOCKE'S THEORY OF MORALITY

1. Catharine Trotter Cockburn. *Catharine Trotter Cockburn: Philosophical Writings.* Peterborough, ON: Broadview Press, 2006: 36.
2. John Locke, "Essays on the Law of Nature," in *Locke: Political Essays*, ed. Mark Goldie. Cambridge: Cambridge University Press, 1977: 82.
3. Ibid., 81.
4. Richard I. Aaron. *John Locke.* Oxford: Clarendon Press, 1971: 257.
5. Locke, "Essays on the Law of Nature," 81.
6. Ibid., 118.
7. Ibid., 105.
8. Ibid., 117.
9. J.B. Schneewind. "Locke's Moral Philosophy," in *The Cambridge Companion to Locke*, ed. Vere Chappell. Cambridge: Cambridge University Press, 1994: 206.

CHAPTER SIX   LOCKE'S THEORY OF KNOWLEDGE

1. Nicholas Jolley has coined the phrase "epistemological individualism" as a means of capturing this private, experiential aspect of Locke's view (Nicholas Jolley, *Locke: His Philosophical Thought* (Oxford: Oxford University Press, 1999): 171).

BIBLIOGRAPHY

WORKS BY LOCKE

Locke, John. *The Correspondence of John Locke*, ed. E.S. De Beer. 4 vols. Oxford: Clarendon Press, 1979.

——. *An Essay Concerning Human Understanding*, ed. Peter Nidditch. Oxford: Clarendon Press, 1975.

——. *Essays on the Law of Nature*, ed. W. von Leyden. Oxford: Clarendon Press, 1954.

——. *John Locke: Drafts for the Essay Concerning Human Understanding and Other Philosophical Writings*, ed. P.H. Nidditch and G.A.J. Rogers. Oxford: Clarendon Press, 1990.

——. *John Locke: Selected Correspondence*, ed. Mark Goldie. Oxford: Oxford University Press, 2002.

——. *Locke: Political Essays*, ed. Mark Goldie. Cambridge: Cambridge University Press, 1997.

——. *Some Familiar Letters between Mr. Locke, and Several of His Friends*. London: for A. and J. Churchill, 1708.

——. *Two Treatises of Government*, ed. Peter Laslett. New York: New American Library, 1965.

——. *The Works of John Locke*, 10 vols. London: Thomas Tegg, 1823; reprinted Aalen: Scientia, 1963.

BIOGRAPHIES

Cranston, M. *John Locke: A Biography*. Oxford: Oxford University Press, 1985.

Milton, J.R. "Locke's Life and Times," in *The Cambridge Companion to Locke*, ed. Vere Chappell. Cambridge: Cambridge University Press, 1994: 5–25.

Rogers, G.A.J. "The Intellectual Setting and Aims of the *Essay*," in *The Cambridge Companion to Locke's "Essay Concerning Human Understanding,"* ed. Lex Newman. Cambridge: Cambridge University Press, 2007: 7–32.

Woolhouse, Roger. *Locke: A Biography*. Cambridge: Cambridge University Press, 2007.

GENERAL SURVEYS

Aaron, Richard I. *John Locke*. Oxford: Clarendon Press, 1971.

Ashcraft, Richard (ed.). *John Locke: Critical Assessments*, vol. 2. New York: Routledge, 1991.

Ayers, Michael. *Locke: Epistemology and Ontology*. London: Routledge, 1991.

Bennett, Jonathan. *Locke, Berkeley, Hume: Central Themes*. Oxford: Oxford University Press, 1971.

Chappell, Vere (ed.). *The Cambridge Companion to Locke*. Cambridge: Cambridge University Press, 1994.

——. *Locke*. Oxford: Oxford University Press, 1998.

Emmanuel, Steven M. *The Blackwell Guide to the Modern Philosophers: From Descartes to Nietzsche*. Malden, MA: Blackwell, 2001.

Hoffman, Paul, Owen, David, and Yaffe, Gideon (eds.). *Contemporary Perspectives on Early Modern Philosophy: Essays in Honor of Vere Chappell*. Peterborough, ON: Broadview Press, 2008.

Jolley, Nicholas. *Locke: His Philosophical Thought*. Oxford: Oxford University Press, 1999.

Lowe, E.J. *Locke on Human Understanding*. New York: Routledge, 1995.

Mackie, J.L. *Problems from Locke*. Oxford: Clarendon Press, 1976.

Newman, Lex (ed.). *The Cambridge Companion to Locke's "Essay Concerning Human Understanding."* Cambridge: Cambridge University Press, 2007.

Rogers, G.A.J. (ed.). *Locke's Philosophy: Content and Context*. Oxford: Clarendon Press, 1994.

Yolton, John. *John Locke: Problems and Perspectives*. Cambridge: Cambridge University Press, 1969.

LOCKE'S THEORY OF IDEAS

Alexander, Peter. *Ideas, Qualities, and Corpuscles: Locke and Boyle on the External World*. Cambridge: Cambridge University Press, 1985.

Bolton, Martha Brandt. "The Taxonomy of Ideas in Locke's *Essay*," in *The Cambridge Companion to Locke's "Essay Concerning Human Understanding,"* ed. Lex Newman. Cambridge: Cambridge University Press, 2007: 67–100.

Chappell, Vere. "Locke's Theory of Ideas," in *The Cambridge Companion to Locke*, ed. Vere Chappell. Cambridge: Cambridge University Press, 1994: 26–55.

Clifford, W.K. *The Scientific Basis of Morals*. New York: Humboldt Publishing Company, 1884.

Cudworth, Ralph. *The True Intellectual System of the Universe*, vol. 2. New York: Gould and Newman, 1838.

Jacovides, Michael. "Locke's Distinctions between Primary and Secondary Qualities," in *The Cambridge Companion to Locke's "Essay Concerning Human Understanding,"* ed. Lex Newman. Cambridge: Cambridge University Press, 2007: 101–129.

Rickless, Samuel C. "Locke's Polemic against Nativism," in *The Cambridge Companion to Locke's "Essay Concerning Human Understanding,"* ed. Lex Newman. Cambridge: Cambridge University Press, 2007: 33–66.

Smith, John. *Select Discourses*. Cambridge: Cambridge University Press, 1859.

Stillingfleet, Edward. *Origines Sacrae*. Oxford: Clarendon Press, 1797.

Yolton, John. *John Locke and the Way of Ideas*. Oxford: Oxford University Press, 1956.

——. "Ideas and Knowledge in Seventeenth-Century Philosophy." *Journal of the History of Philosophy*, 13 (1975): 373–388.

——. *Perceptual Acquaintance: From Descartes to Reid*. Minneapolis: University of Minnesota Press, 1984.

LOCKE'S THEORY OF MATTER

Atherton, Margaret. "Knowledge of Substance and Knowledge of Science in Locke's *Essay*." *History of Philosophy Quarterly*, 1 (1984): 413–427.

Ayers, Michael. "The Foundations of Knowledge and the Logic of Substance: The Structure of Locke's General Philosophy," in *Locke's Philosophy: Content and Context*, ed. G.A.J. Rogers. Oxford: Clarendon Press, 1994: 49–74.

Bennett, Jonathan. "Substratum." *History of Philosophy Quarterly*, 4 (1987): 197–215.

Bolton, Martha Brandt. "The Origins of Locke's Doctrine of Primary and Secondary Qualities." *Philosophical Quarterly*, 26 (1976): 305–316.

——. "Substances, Substrata, and Names of Substances in Locke's *Essay*." *Philosophical Review*, 85 (1976): 488–513.

——. "The Real Molyneux Question and the Basis of Locke's Answer," in *Locke's Philosophy: Content and Context*, ed. G.A.J. Rogers. Oxford: Clarendon Press, 1994: 75–100.

Curley, Edwin. "Locke, Boyle, and the Distinction between Primary and Secondary Qualities." *Philosophical Review*, 81 (1972): 438–464.

McCann, Edwin. "Locke's Philosophy of Body," in *The Cambridge Companion to Locke*, ed. Vere Chappell. Cambridge: Cambridge University Press, 1994: 56–88.

——. "Locke on Substance," in *The Cambridge Companion to Locke's "Essay Concerning Human Understanding,"* ed. Lex Newman. Cambridge: Cambridge University Press, 2007: 157–191.

LOCKE'S THEORY OF LANGUAGE

Atherton, Margaret. "Locke on Essences and Classification," in *The Cambridge Companion to Locke's "Essay Concerning Human Understanding,"* ed. Lex Newman. Cambridge: Cambridge University Press, 2007: 258–285.

Ashworth, E.J. "Locke on Language." *Canadian Journal of Philosophy*, 14 (1984): 45–74.

——. "Do Words Signify Ideas or Things? The Scholastic Sources of Locke's Theory of Language." *Journal of the History of Philosophy*, 19 (1981): 299–326.

Guyer, Paul. "Locke's Philosophy of Language," in *The Cambridge Companion to Locke*, ed. Vere Chappell. Cambridge: Cambridge University Press, 1994: 115–145.

Landesman, Charles. "Locke's Theory of Meaning," in *John Locke: Critical Assessments*, vol. 2, ed. Richard Ashcraft. New York: Routledge, 1991: 218–234.

Losonsky, Michael. "Locke on Meaning and Signification," in *Locke's Philosophy: Content and Context*, ed. G.A.J. Rogers. Oxford: Clarendon Press, 1994: 123–142.

———. *Linguistic Turns in Modern Philosophy*. Cambridge: Cambridge University Press, 2006.

———. "Language, Meaning, and Mind in Locke's *Essay*," in *The Cambridge Companion to Locke's "Essay Concerning Human Understanding,"* ed. Lex Newman. Cambridge: Cambridge University Press, 2007: 286–312.

Mill, John Stuart. *A System of Logic, Ratiocinative and Inductive*. London: Longmans, Green and Co., 1884.

LOCKE'S THEORY OF IDENTITY

Barber, K.F. and Garcia, J.J.E. *Individuation and Identity in Early Modern Philosophy*. Albany: State University of New York Press, 1994.

Butler, Joseph. *Analogy of Religion*. New York: Harper & Brothers, 1860.

Hume, David. *A Treatise of Human Nature*, ed. P.H. Nidditch. Oxford: Clarendon Press, 1978.

McCann, Edwin. "Locke on Identity: Matter, Life, and Consciousness," in *The Empiricists: Critical Essays on Locke, Berkeley, and Hume*, ed. Margaret Atherton. New York: Rowman & Littlefield, 1998: 63–88.

———. "Identity, Essentialism, and the Substance of Body in Locke," in *Contemporary Perspectives on Early Modern Philosophy: Essays in Honor of Vere Chappell*, ed. Paul Hoffman, David Owen and Gideon Yaffe. Peterborough, ON: Broadview Press, 2008: 173–190.

Molyneux, William. "Letter of December 23, 1693," in *Some Familiar Letters between Mr. Locke, and Several of His Friends*. London: for A. and J. Churchill, 1708.

Noonan, Harold W. "Locke on Personal Identity," in *"An Essay Concerning Human Understanding" in Focus*, ed. Gary Fuller, Robert Stecker, and John P. Wright. London: Routledge, 2000: 210–235.

Yaffe, Gideon. "Locke on Ideas of Identity and Diversity," in *The Cambridge Companion to Locke's "Essay Concerning Human Understanding,"* ed. Lex Newman. Cambridge: Cambridge University Press, 2007: 192–230.

LOCKE'S THEORY OF MORALITY

Chappell, Vere. "Locke on the Freedom of the Will," in *Locke's Philosophy: Content and Context*, ed. G.A.J. Rogers. Oxford: Clarendon Press, 1994: 101–121.

———. "Locke on the Suspension of Desire." *Locke Newsletter*, 29 (1998): 23–38.

BIBLIOGRAPHY

Cockburn, Catharine Trotter. *Catharine Trotter Cockburn: Philosophical Writings*. Peterborough, ON: Broadview Press, 2006.

Colman, John. *John Locke's Moral Philosophy*. Edinburgh: Edinburgh University Press, 1983.

Darwall, Stephen. *The British Moralists and the Internal "Ought": 1640–1740*. Cambridge: Cambridge University Press, 1995.

Lamprecht, S. *The Moral and Political Philosophy of John Locke*. New York: Columbia University Press, 1962.

Schneewind, J.B. "Locke's Moral Philosophy," in *The Cambridge Companion to Locke*, ed. Vere Chappell. Cambridge: Cambridge University Press, 1994: 199–225.

———. *The Invention of Autonomy*. Cambridge: Cambridge University Press, 1998.

Sheridan, Patricia. "Pirates, Kings and Reasons to Act: Moral Motivation and the Role of Sanctions in Locke's Moral Theory." *Canadian Journal of Philosophy*, 37 (2007): 35–48.

———. "Reflection, Nature, and Moral Law: The Extent of Catharine Cockburn's Lockeanism in Her *Defence of Mr. Locke's* Essay." *Hypatia*, 22 (2007): 133–151.

Wilson, Catherine. "The Moral Epistemology of Locke's *Essay*," in *The Cambridge Companion to Locke's "Essay Concerning Human Understanding,"* ed. Lex Newman. Cambridge: Cambridge University Press, 2007: 381–405.

Wolterstorff, Nicholas. *John Locke and the Ethics of Belief*. Cambridge: Cambridge University Press, 1996.

LOCKE'S THEORY OF KNOWLEDGE

Jolley, Nicholas. "Locke on Faith and Reason," in *The Cambridge Companion to Locke's "Essay Concerning Human Understanding,"* ed. Lex Newman. Cambridge: Cambridge University Press, 2007: 436–455.

Newman, Lex. "Locke on Knowledge," in *The Cambridge Companion to Locke's "Essay Concerning Human Understanding,"* ed. Lex Newman. Cambridge: Cambridge University Press, 2007: 313–351.

Owen, David. "Locke on Judgment," in *The Cambridge Companion to Locke's "Essay Concerning Human Understanding,"* ed. Lex Newman. Cambridge: Cambridge University Press, 2007: 406–435.

Wolterstorff, Nicholas. "Locke's Philosophy of Religion," in *The Cambridge Companion to Locke*, ed. Vere Chappell. Cambridge: Cambridge University Press, 1994: 172–198.

Woolhouse, Roger. "Locke's Theory of Knowledge," in *The Cambridge Companion to Locke*, ed. Vere Chappell. Cambridge: Cambridge University Press, 1994: 146–171.

EARLY-MODERN SCIENCE

Bacon, Francis. *The New Organon*, ed. Lisa Jardine and Michael Silverthorne. Cambridge: Cambridge University Press, 2000.

Boyle, Robert. *Selected Philosophical Papers of Robert Boyle*, ed. M.A. Stewart. Manchester: Manchester University Press, 1979.

——. *The Excellencies of Robert Boyle*, ed. J.J. MacIntosh. Peterborough, ON: Broadview Press, 2008.

Lennon, Thomas. *The Battle of the Gods and Giants*. Princeton, NJ: Princeton University Press, 1993.

Mandelbaum, M. *Philosophy, Science and Sense Perception*. Baltimore, MD: Johns Hopkins University Press, 1964.

Matthews, Michael R. (ed.). *The Scientific Background to Modern Philosophy*. Indianapolis, IN: Hackett, 1989.

Wilson, Catherine. *The Invisible World: Early Modern Philosophy and the Invention of the Microscope*. Princeton, NJ: Princeton University Press, 1995.

FURTHER READING

WORKS BY LOCKE

The standard edition of the *Essay* is considered by most scholars to be the Nidditch edition cited in the Bibliography. There are numerous other editions of Locke's *Essay*, many of them abridged. An excellent example of the latter is the *In Focus* edition published by Routledge, which includes an abridged version of the *Essay* and four articles dealing with major issues in the *Essay* written by leading Locke scholars. Since the *Essay* went through a number of drafts, with some significant alterations, it is useful for anyone undertaking a serious study of Locke to consult earlier incarnations of this work. *John Locke: Drafts for the Essay Concerning Human Understanding and Other Philosophical Writings*, edited by P.H. Nidditch and G.A.J. Rogers, is an excellent resource in this regard.

An excellent collection of Locke's political writings and other essays is Goldie's *Locke: Political Essays*. This is a valuable resource for anyone interested in Locke's political and moral writing. Goldie has also edited a collection of Locke's correspondence (cited in the Bibliography). A full collection of Locke's correspondence is also available in four volumes, edited by De Beer. Locke's *Essays on the Law of Nature* is available in translation from the original Latin, edited by von Leyden. This work is especially important for studies in Locke's moral philosophy.

SECONDARY READING

There are a number of very good general works on Locke's philosophy as well as a number of edited volumes regarding aspects of Locke's thought. Of the former, three of the most accessible for readers new to Locke are Aaron's *John Locke*, Lowe's *Locke on Human Understanding* and Jolley's *Locke: His Philosophical Thought*.

Undeniably, Ayers's work *Locke: Epistemology and Ontology* is a landmark study of Locke's philosophy. While this work may be difficult for readers new to Locke, it is one of most significant works on Locke published in recent years. Ayers's interpretation of Locke's text, while at times controversial, has made Ayers one of the leading Locke scholars today.

There are also a number of excellent edited volumes containing papers by some of the major names in Locke scholarship. While there are too many to list here, two very good collections have come out in the *Cambridge Companion* series. The first is *The Cambridge Companion to Locke*, edited by Chappell. The second, and more recent, is *The Cambridge Companion to Locke's "Essay Concerning Human Understanding,"* edited by Newman. Both volumes are excellent resources for research on Locke's philosophical writing, introducing the reader to a number of debates regarding the interpretation of Locke through the work of some of the most highly respected Locke scholars. Other works, notably by Ashcraft and Yolton, are also strongly recommended and contain some groundbreaking scholarship on Locke. This list is not by any means exhaustive; it is intended only to point the reader to some of the better-known publications of this sort available.

BACKGROUND TO THE *ESSAY*

A number of notable works provide the reader with a general understanding of the intellectual backdrop for the *Essay*. Yolton's *John Locke and the Way of Ideas* is considered a classic piece of scholarship on Locke, locating Locke's theory of ideas within the debates of his time. Alexander's book *Ideas, Qualities, and Corpuscles: Locke and Boyle on the External World* provides a good understanding of the scientific developments that influenced Locke's writing. Also notable in this regard are Mandelbaum's *Philosophy, Science and Sense Perception* and Wilson's *The Invisible World: Early Modern Philosophy and the Invention of the Microscope*. For an excellent collection of scientific writings that were greatly influential in Locke's period, see Matthews's *The Scientific Background to Modern Philosophy*. Lennon's work *The Battle of the Gods and Giants* is also a very useful examination of the competing worldviews that shaped early-modern thinking.

Barber and Garcia's work *Individuation and Identity in Early Modern Philosophy* is a study of the concepts of individuation of identity across a number of philosophers of Locke's period. For Locke's moral philosophy, see Schneewind's *The Invention of Autonomy*, Colman's *John Locke's Moral Philosophy* and Darwall's *The British Moralists and the Internal "Ought": 1640–1740*. These three works have all made significant contributions to our understanding of Locke's moral theory and provide a very useful context for understanding Locke's moral views. Emmanuel's *The Blackwell Guide to the Modern Philosophers: From Descartes to Nietzsche* offers the reader a good understanding of the major thinkers and ideas of Locke's period.

INDEX

as source of words 52
extra-mental objects
  ideas and 19–20
  justificatory reasons for the
    existence 105–6, 108

faith 115–18
forms
  language and 55
  Platonist account 55
  Scholastic–Aristotelian
    view 35–6, 37, 42

general terms 55
  Aristotelian notion 60
  Locke's notion 58–63
  origin 42–5
Glorious Revolution 7
God
  innatist theory 9–11
  Molyneux's drunken criminal
    example 75–6
  righteousness 98
  see also divine laws; faith
good and evil 91–2
government
  definition 88

Harvey, William 6
hedonism
  morality and 84–5, 90–2, 97–8
Hobbes, Thomas 5, 87
human identity 70–1, 79, 80
  forensic distinction between
    personal and 73–4, 77
human understanding
  limits 17–18
Hume, David
  identity theory 79–80
  rationalism of 87
  substantial unity of 41–2, 43, 45
Huygens, Christiaan 6

ideas
  adverbial theory 20–1

empiricist notion 86, 87
Locke's definition 17
Locke's theory 16–18, 64
Locke's theory, sense and
  reference in 52–4
origin and nature 2–3, 17
representational thesis
  19–20, 21
identity
  Cartesian 65
  conditions for 69–71
  Corpuscularian view 65–6
  essentialist view 68
  Hume's theory 79–80
  Locke's theory 65–8
  Locke's theory, critique of
    75–8
  Scholastic–Aristotelian
    view 65
individuation
  identity and 66–8
inert bodies
  identity conditions 69
injustice 88
  social 95
innateness
  critical inquiry and 28
  identity and 66
  Locke's arguments against
    11–16
  moderate theory 10–11
  morality and 85
  naïve theory 9–10, 11
  rationalist view 86
inquiry 2–4
intuitive evidence 102
intuitive knowledge 102–3

James II, *King of England* 7
judgments 24
  idea association and 30–2
  knowledge *vs.* 101–2
  perception and 24–5, 26–7
  probable knowledge and 112–15
justice 63, 89, 110

INDEX